COPPERNICKEL

number 21 / fall 2015

EDITOR/MANAGING EDITOR
Wayne Miller

EDITORS: POETRY
Brian Barker
Nicky Beer

EDITOR: FICTION
Teague Bohlen

EDITOR: FICTION & NONFICTION
Joanna Luloff

SENIOR EDITOR
Courtney Harrell

ASSOCIATE EDITORS
Steven Dawson
Emily Jessen
Jennifer Loyd
Lyn Poats
Kyra Scrimgeour

EDITORIAL INTERNS
Haleigh Canalte
Meredith Herndon

ASSISTANT EDITORS
Alison Auger
Angela Bogart-Monteith
Erin Brackett
Joseph Carrillo
Karl Chwe
Maggie Gelbwaks
Jacqueline Gallegos
Kylee Gomez
Kimberlie Grady
Sammi Johnson
Taylor Kirby
Hannah Miles

Andrew Nellis
Conner North
Scott Overbey
Laura-Joy Salter
Ashlynn Soresi

CONTRIBUTING EDITORS
Robert Archambeau
Mark Brazaitis
Geoffrey Brock
A. Papatya Bucak
Victoria Chang
Martha Collins
Robin Ekiss
Tarfia Faizullah
V. V. Ganeshananthan
Kevin Haworth
Joy Katz
David Keplinger
Jesse Lee Kercheval
Jason Koo
Thomas Legendre
Randall Mann
Adrian Matejka
Pedro Ponce
Kevin Prufer
Frederick Reiken
James Richardson
Emily Ruskovich
Eliot Khalil Wilson

ART CONSULTANTS
Maria Elena Buszek
Adam Lerner

OFFICE MANAGERS
Elaine Beemer
Francine Olivas-Zarate

COPPERNICKEL

Copper Nickel is the national literary journal housed at the University of Colorado Denver. Published in March and September, it features poetry, fiction, essays, and work in translation by established and emerging writers. We welcome submissions from all writers. Submissions are assumed to be original and unpublished. For more information, please visit copper-nickel.org. Subscriptions are available—and at discounted rates for students—at regonline.com/coppernickelsubscriptions. *Copper Nickel* is distributed to subscribers and through Publishers Group West and Media Solutions. We are deeply grateful for the support of the Department of English and the College of Liberal Arts & Sciences at the University of Colorado Denver.

CONTENTS

POETRY

TRANSLATION FOLIOS

On the Cover / Mark Mothersbaugh, *Untitled*, Ink on paper, 2013

(for more about Mark Mothersbaugh's visual art,
visit markmothersbaughart.com)

Editor's Note:

IN CONJUNCTION WITH OUR RELAUNCH, *Copper Nickel* will now offer two $500 Editors' Prizes—one in poetry, one in prose—for the most exciting work in each issue, as determined by a vote of our editorial staff. Results will be announced in the subsequent issue, as well as via social media and the *Copper Nickel* website. The winners for issue 20 were Michelle Oakes for her poems "Bionics" and "How to Live" and Donovan Ortega for his essay "In a Large Coastal City." Congratulations to both writers!

—Wayne Miller

DAVID HERNANDEZ

Algebra of the Sky

I am bored with all this emptiness, God said,
I will create myself, words, utter *I am*
bored with all this emptiness, but first
I must create emptiness, then myself,
consciousness, boredom, finally
language. Or did I engineer myself
before emptiness? God wondered. Weird
that I conceived wondering, too.
Alright, time to carve the matchstick,
braid the fuse, ignite the extravagant
boom, this will be the beginning
of everything, although I was
here before that, busy stacking black
and soundless blocks of nothingness,
holding back my yawning. But who
built me? God thought. Shoot, I forgot:
me. Without a blueprint, I made my hands
to make my hands make myself. It is so
confusing, it being language, language being
the lanyard knots to my thinking. I was here
before there was a here, it's that simple,
it's that mystifying, a clear explanation
hides inside the oblong shadow
my zero casts. God pondered. I am done
trying to solve it, the whittled matchstick is
waiting, the ponytailed fuse is waiting,
here come the pyrotechnics, let those
long away from this moment
tip their minds to a tightlipped sky
and figure it out.

KEITH LEONARD

Conceiving the Child

I wanted to say a word of praise
and for that word to grow suddenly
physical. There was a tingling
in the cellar and I wanted to sketch
the image squirreled in the dark.
I know little of the crude mechanics
which double us, but I wanted
the blunt eloquence gripping my finger.
The everyday lyric. Impossible
as winding a clock with my throat's
green fiddle, strange as planting
a whole grassy range if I sneezed,
I am spellbound—spellbound—
by what the body will dream.

KATHRYN NUERNBERGER

The Invention of the Hunter

In the time when crows were as white as doves, there was an egg cracked open by lightning strike and the bird that emerged from that egg could not sing, could only caw. Such raw-throated barking can only make an animal angry and mean. This crow made a game for herself of finding a rabbit den and perching atop it to caw until every creature in the hole was made to meat. If one tried to slip out the back way, she'd follow it over the wood to perch atop the next den and the next. Sometimes a rabbit just collapsed in the middle of a leap, dead of its own running.

Now this kind of crow lays only one egg in the whole of her life and that egg will not hatch, but the mother must peck it open herself, and what's inside is a tucked-up human, naked and waiting.

LAURA STOTT

Monster

Spider webs by the backdoor funnel into
a black cave, a silk and nocturnal universe
where a fanged creature waits
for the moon's threaded children—
a moth, a marbled wasp—
to crawl gently into the tangle
of reflection.

Mother spider wraps her eight legs lovingly
around all her young and whispers,
this is the earth
you are waiting to be born into—
dream of the wings you'll eat,
and kingdoms between roses.

ANNA B. SUTTON

Gemini

A two-headed dolphin pup washed up
on the shore—pink heads split like legs
opening. Two dead mouths smiling

where I expected feet. A single fin stiff
with weeds. Conjoined couplet—color of
nail beds, early melon—be sure, there are

as many horrors in the ocean as there are
on land. I can't stand to think of you alive
for even a moment after spilling out into

the saltwater, struggling to swim while
your mother made the grim decision to leave.
I hope you were gone long before then, hope

holding each other close in the womb—inverse
of the ocean: warm, shallow, and sugar-sweet—
a chorus of blood and breath sung you to sleep.

TYLER MILLS

Front

THE SELF MUST EXPLORE A thing until it screams. As a child, I would sit in the grass, touching the cold tufts with my fingers. *Dig, dig, dig.* I made a fist-sized hole. Inside it, a gray worm flipped over, curling like a question mark.

I would scream at the worm. I would scream at the hole I made. I would scream at what was inside it.

The self can be a receptacle.

The mouth takes everything in.

•

BATMAN, OBVIOUSLY NOT MY HUSBAND'S name, and I always joke about gunshots when firecrackers are launched in May, June, July, August, and September in our Chicago neighborhood on the west side.

Batman likes to walk me to the L when I'm leaving for an early flight at 4:00 AM. He rolls my suitcase over the curb. Bump. Bump. At the exact moment when the wheels skipped concrete, we heard two gunshots explode the shadows from the trees.

With his arm, he barred me from moving forward. The echo came from a block away—the McDonalds parking lot. Sometimes, during gang initiation season, two men in white will chase a third man through the L cars. On the platform, I once saw two men try to push the third over the edge. This happened at rush hour in the morning.

I'd never really heard a gun go off like this: I've heard the stray shot of hunters in the forest when I played at my friend's house in the country. Those guns made me think of crows scaring off a roof. It frightened me still.

The sound is like your neighbor screaming at your friend in the backyard. Profane in its proximity to the swing set, your friend paling blank-faced as the wall of a warehouse.

It splits time for a second.

Batman and I paused, and so did a bicyclist coming home from somewhere—bartending? The sun would rise in two hours. He was about to cross the intersection in front of us, but he stopped and touched the toes of his Converse sneakers to the road. His bike made a clicking sound, and the wheels turned into the gravel of a pothole. We all looked around.

"Hey . . . shit," I found myself saying. The bicyclist slowly started backing up his bike, still on his toes. Then he pedaled it out of there and disappeared.

"Let's go," said Batman.

I didn't want to go. I wanted to find out what was going on. "What *happened?*" I asked, not him, but the night, I suppose. I broke free of Batman's hold. Reason took over.

"It'll be too late to check this bag if we go around the block. I'm going to be late," I said.

I stepped toward the road and looked down it.

"No," said Batman.

•

MY MIND SOMETIMES RENAMES PLACES. Corner of Weed Wolf Graffiti Stickers. Pepsi Man's Curb. Daffodil Boulevard. One afternoon, after Batman and I had a minor argument—I wasn't sleeping well—I grabbed Charles Wright's *Zone Journals* off the shelf and took a walk: past the Grecian Statue, the Blind Corner, and Red Light Number 1. I joined the community of bums in the park between two roads. They were here a lot. Today, they were sharing a long yellow bottle. I decided to sit on a bench that faced away from the road. When I sat down, I noticed white graffiti arrows on the path that pointed at the seat. Oh well.

I opened my book. People walked their dogs through the grass. I wanted a dog. Then it caught my eye, a blocky white symbol. Someone had sprayed a different, frazzled purple symbol over it. I lined up my sandals with the arrow points. One, two. The symbols near them reminded me of when my little sister would copy my signature. The sunlight warmed my arms.

A man in a ripped T-shirt walked by, whistling. He slowed down.

I wondered if I had become part of a pattern of some kind. I had recently realized the apartment building on our corner was a major distribution center. The vans came on Thursdays. I would cross the street and then cross back. I was followed home once, but nothing happened. The two men, really young men, just watched me as I keyed into my apartment.

I stood up, stretching. My bench was the only one labeled with symbols.

•

I'M TOUCHING A SHEET OF TULLE threaded with gold plastic beads.

The cloth hangs above me. The cloth is deep purple, not quite plum. The room is lined with curtain displays. Like the one in front of me.

The curtains cover the perimeter of the room and also create alleys through it. I am standing at the farthest edge from the door. I like the plum one. It looks like a magician's curtain.

I put my face to the sheen.

A whisper of material. The creases still accordion-edged where the cloth had been folded inside its plastic packet. I think about putting my palms on the Corinthian columns of a museum.

Someone screams. A girl is standing by the front window.

Gunshots. Two.

Men's voices.

I slip behind the magic scrim.

I admire the cloth from inside of it. My back presses against the concrete wall behind me. The curtain is just opaque enough.

Men stamp through the aisles. Five or six, I would guess. I can see them even though I am layered outside of perception.

And now I can see them from above, as though I'm clinging to one of the curtain rods and looking straight down.

The curtain barely touches my mouth.

The curtain feels like the hair of someone sleeping next to you, strange, different, almost yours. It wakes me. My husband's hair brushes my mouth.

·

THERE IS ACTUALLY SUCH A thing as a cloak that removes you from time.

Batman explained this to me while he washed knives.

You can slip the cloak over your body and walk across a room.

You can stay inside the cloak as long as you like. When you slip into it, no one will see you. Then you will be seen again, reappearing next to the stove a breath later.

Your body is erased, zapped, swallowed by a hole.

The light will receive your body.

Then, your body will block the light, and you will re-enter the world.

·

I'M TOUCHING A SHEET OF tulle threaded with gold plastic beads. The cloth hangs above me. My mother is touching another curtain next to this one, talking about how she would like to use it in a weaving she is making. She is an artist.

"I could do a lot with this," she says. Her glasses are pushed on top of her head.

"Why don't you get it?"

"It has to be juuust right…" She inspects the hem.

Because my apartment doesn't yet have a shower curtain, or a shower curtain rod, or window curtains, my mother thought we should check out Dollar Linen on Milwaukee Ave. on our way back from the bakery. I love dollar stores. So does she. My family would buy Christmas gifts for each other at the Dollar Store next to the Aldi's when I was growing up.

Dollar Linen takes up two Chicago storefronts. Rugs hang in the window.

One half of the store, which could be a store in itself, is devoted to every possible household item. Drain plugs. Salad spinners. Juicers. Sets of picnic plates. And toys. Plastic doll heads that you can fit onto doll bodies. Feathered felt spiked with catnip. And toiletries. And cocoa butter. And candles of any scent. Candles with images of the Virgin Mary on them and prayers printed up the sides. My mother bought a Virgin Mary candle for me to burn.

When Batman and I first started seeing each other, back when we lived in Maryland, we walked from my apartment complex to the dollar store in the nearby strip mall in one of the D.C. suburbs. At the Dollar Store, we bought weird greeting cards for our mutual friend, who was driving to Georgia for her uncle's funeral. We laughed about how the cards said something a little wrong. We thought she'd laugh, too.

Congratulations! May your Riches Bring you Friendship.

Enjoy Retirement. You have the Rest of Your Life.

She liked the retirement card.

As we walked down the aisles, my mother and I ran our hands through robin's egg gauze, through butter yellow taffeta, through swaths of cotton spotted with cherries, and through lace tiebacks hanging up alone like ribbons lost from a dress.

On the way out the front door, she stopped at the cashier.

"You have a very nice place. What are your hours?" she asked.

"Thank you, Madam." With formality, the man handed us each a laminated business card. I could smell incense burning: cedar and raspberry. A man without teeth smiled at us and bowed his head as we crossed the threshold into the bright afternoon.

•

THE LAST TIME I WENT to Dollar Linen was because of a sign scrawled on the window:

We Cut Keys

It was winter.

"Hello. May I help you?"

It was the man who stood near the door. He wheezed. I noticed he was missing many teeth.

"Do you sell cat food?" I asked.

I took off my mittens.

The man opened his mouth in surprise. The winter wind on his gums must have cut to the nerve. I was wearing two pairs of pants and a hat under the hood of my coat.

"Cat food?" He stepped closer to me. "You don't want to get that here."

"Oh. OK."

He looked down at my mittens. One thumb was beginning to unravel.

"Do you have drain traps?"

"Yes, yes. Follow me, Madam."

This store had *everything*. Roach traps in S, M, L. Hand towels dyed in red spots: prints that tomatoes make when hurled at a garage. The toothless man led me down one of the aisles along the room's edge. I could hear my boots scuffing the linoleum floor. There were no sounds, not even the radio. If I were by myself, I would have cut straight down the center of the room. The back door was in the center of the room.

I thought of my body cutting through the air.

Some guys appeared: they sauntered toward us.

"Thanks." The man's eyes were red.

"Good day, sir," responded my guide. He turned to me. "This?" he asked me and pointed to a series of hooks.

There were four different drain traps hanging on the wall. We were in the back of the room.

I felt warm and unzipped my coat. I loosened the scarf at my throat, and chose two traps (one was $1.00, and the other $1.75).

Then, my guide led me to the front, where I could smell the incense. I put the traps on the cashier's counter. I asked about having some keys cut. The cashier took my key ring from my hands and marked the two I wanted copied with a Sharpie. I didn't like that. He turned away, and the machine began.

In the machine, my keys made a shrill, grinding noise: it reminded me of that sound of bones being run through a wood-chipper from *Fargo*.

"It sure is cold out," I said.

"Yes, yes."

The machine ground and ground.

"But it is nice and warm in here!" I said. I don't know why I said that.

The man without teeth walked briskly toward the door. A kid walked in. The kid was wearing a puffy Blackhawks coat that touched his knees. He must have been twelve, and in his older brother's jacket. Or, maybe it had always been his. The toothless man was happy to see him. They shook hands and laughed.

The child's skin was pocked. His eyes were red. The two of them disappeared for a moment, and when they reappeared the boy was putting something into his pocket. I stared, and the cashier caught me.

"Yes, it's warm. My poor heating bill!" he said in mock good humor, his voice lilting. But his were eyes sharp as he looked up at me from his work.

"Oh, yes! I can only imagine!" I sung. The shriek of the key-cutter cut out just as I began to speak. "Heat is so expensive these days."

It was like I was projecting to an empty theatre.

I felt like a fool, making this kind of conversation. Who says, "Heat is so expensive these days?"

For a moment, the cashier held up both sets of my keys: the thicker, copper-colored ones my landlord handed me in August, and the shinny new gold ones.

His fingertips played with the new keys, the ones he made, showing the metal to the light.

I remembered the men that kept coming to the front of the store from a room in the back. I noticed I was the only woman there. I noticed no one else was buying anything. I realized there was always a man on lookout at the front door. I thought about how the plastic cups, the dolls, the candy, all of it looked old: some of it dusty. I thought about my comment, about the heat. How did Dollar Linen pay to heat the building? I remembered the men that kept coming to the front of the store from a room in the back.

I looked around. The cashier watched me look around.

Get out, a voice said. It wasn't my voice, but it was inside me.

It's the voice that said *Stand up* when two men sat, one in front and one next to me, on an empty train car of the D.C. metro.

Sometimes the voice has a form. It pushes you, gently, to the door of the train and onto the platform when you need to go. There is a shift in atmosphere, and you feel the gentle push on your back. *Back up.*

Stop digging at it. The thing. Stop thinking about it, wondering about it. See the hole? Stop it. You will dig something up. You will dig up the thing that exists out of sight. The thing that coils around the roots of it all.

The Midwestern sky sometimes stripes with clouds so high that it feels like we are inside a giant bowl.

It is headache bright.

One day, the sky will be just like this: glaucoma blue.

Listen. You might not believe it, but there is such a thing as a scrim. One day you will rip it.

You will fight against the hands pushing you to walk away. Goodbye, Batman. You'll take a shortcut.

The sky—I want to say it will rip, too. That the epiphany will dissolve. That there won't be one. That the shadows aren't already making lace of your arms.

Translation Folio

YI LU

Translator's Introduction

Fiona Sze-Lorrain

Yɪ Lᴜ ɪs ᴀ Cʜɪɴᴇsᴇ woman poet born in 1956 in Fujian province of southern China. Beyond the one-paragraph biography as an introduction, little is revealed about her life. The private poet, however, stands as a voice of its own, associated with neither a movement nor school of thought—certainly not under the flagship of political endorsement. This is no easy task, considering the context of a Communist state whose history and culture are engendered by Confucian ethics, Maoist discourse, and collective consciousness. Over years, her work has steadily found its readership because of consistency and an engagement with ecology through language.

Currently a resident in urban Fuzhou, the capital city of Fujian, Yi Lu is a theater scenographer and set designer by profession. By extension, virtually all her poems here carry a statement on, or illustration of, nature. Such is her call to arms for an aesthetic to reflect this identity—not by deference, but of belonging—the transcendance of a mortal existence in this universe. But Yi Lu is a reticent artist; to see Yi as a spokesperson for ecological causes undercuts the lyrical vitality of the poems. For her, writing functions more as an experience of feeling *chez soi* than the endeavor of creating another home. Without sentimentalism, or extravagant verbalism, her work speaks, in an image-driven language, to the transience of matter. I consider Yi Lu a quiet poet who says something "shapeful" yet precise. To question the role of a (post-)modern human existence in a larger cosmos, she evokes and invokes nature in its grandeur or small moments, but with a philosophically inquiring mind. Take a look at "Heavy Rain," in which the poet recalls her deceased father and thinks of his tombstone without directly involving her own grief—a "worldly suffering"—as she looks to rain and an otherworldliness:

> are there creatures on the wild path
> faces ravaged by water
>
> some things are never kept indoors
> they stay forever in the rain

The author of five collections, Yi Lu began publishing her writings in 1984. The union of nature and symbolic vision—what Yi defines as "the unseen limit"— is a thematic concern in *See* (2004), *Using Two Seas* (2009), and *Forever Lingering* (2011). I translate Yi Lu with gratitude, humbled by her ritual witnessing of the nonhuman.

Her faith in a restorative quiet—hence a gentle lucidity—is as much an inspiration as a refreshing read. All these six poems are forthcoming in *Sea Summit* (Milkweed Editions, 2015)—a bilingual collection that contains my translations of Yi Lu's selected poems over a span of more than two decades.

In an Instant

a hen pecks at rice
its calm fixes the flow of mist
like a locked lake
even dusk can't enter

but I know
this delicate machine
can be opened by a knife
and never reassembled back

a last grain of rice
links to a lost instant
flooded by even more instants

They Still Have Not Emerged

what hides in the magnolia bush
a magpie flew in and did not come out after a long time
a sparrow flapped its wings and flew in, but did not come out
a butterfly emerged and flirted around
flew back in
but has not been out since

wind moves the leaves
the long hall of shadows must be swaying
they still have not emerged

Valley's Green

that valley is a huge dye vat
I just stand on its edge
feel its rich green
oozing from the sole   to toetips   and fingertips
throughout the whole body in an instant
even the heart is sprouting with green
those insects must be green throughout
even voices are like jade pieces
only flowers can't be dyed
all of them like tiny saucers   little bowls   little cups
filled to the brim with their own colors

Marigold

this smallest lake merges with the rising sun
this smallest hall stops rays of light
what perseverance can open them
linking thousands of spring roads
a myriad flow of honey-yellow
how chaotic

bees have sucked away sorrow
golden cups can't hold blind passion
little volcanoes under butterfly bellies
burning is their only expression

silence has said it all
marigold
marigold
shallow abyss shallow

Heavy Rain

heavy rain   strikes the window
I get up to remove clothes hung outside
and look afar
the cement patch on Father's tomb
must be struck aloud

is Father also watching this heavy rain
thinking about worldly suffering
are there creatures on the wild path
faces ravaged by water

some things are never kept indoors
they stay forever in the rain

One Day It Will Stop Completely

there is a small boat in your left chest
sometimes it rocks violently   jerking fibers in arms and back
dragging storms out of big and small blood vessels
shoulder blade like a cape   where white waves break and break

you press it with one palm   then with the other
like placing a rock on a lid
and consoling it breathlessly   *please   don't   God already knows*

it will calm down   firmly stuck inside
sensibly   with no wind sneaking in

one day it will stop completely
boats at sea are riding on waves and wind

Translated from the Chinese by Fiona Sze-Lorrain

POLLY ROSENWAIKE

June

As the baby was growing inside Natalie's uterus, her aunt Dina was dying. It became an awful race: which would happen first, the birth or the death? If the baby came first, that meant Dina could see her, the new life dandled before the one on the way out. Natalie's mother expressed a tearful hope that Dina would hold on long enough to meet her grandniece. Natalie secretly preferred the death to come first, not so it could be followed by a joyous event, but because she didn't want the baby to detract from it. She wasn't a practicing Jew, but she wanted to go into mourning in the old Jewish way: stop everything, tear her clothes, sit around all day for a week with relatives she didn't much like, and accept plates of heavy food she didn't want to eat. How could a newborn fit into that ritual, with the round-the-clock nursing, and the adorable outfits, and the congratulatory emails?

Up late with nausea and worry during her pregnancy, Natalie considered these two lives—Dina and the baby. Which one would she choose? She'd played games like this as an only child in the back seat on long car rides. If just one could be saved—the dog or the cat, her gymnastics team or her Hebrew School class, her mom or her dad—which would it be? While her parents talked to each other about work and bills and other people's problems, she deliberated. By the time they got to Cape Cod, or Ithaca, or Bennington, she had to decide. The dog, the gymnastics team, her dad, Dina.

Dina's son Matt had been born on May 10th, Natalie's half birthday. She was six-and-a-half that year. It was a strange and fascinating fact that on November 10th, when she would forever be turning another year older, Matt would forever be having his half birthday. Maybe, Natalie thought, Matt was a kind of half twin. A woman at the supermarket had asked, wasn't she lonely with no brothers or sisters, and Natalie supposed that she was. She made her new cousin a card with a joke in it. WELCOME MATT, it said, with a picture of a baby boy lying on a rug in front of a red door. She helped her mom pick out a miniature pair of pajamas and a purple stuffed monkey and wrap them in polka-dotted paper. She ran up Aunt Dina and Uncle Rob's driveway with the card and the package in her hand. Dina opened the door, the baby hiding in a blanket against her chest, and Natalie felt suddenly shy.

"Isn't he funny-looking?" Dina asked, tilting the bundle in her arms so that Natalie could see.

"Yes," she said.

"He's precious," her mom protested. But Matt looked more like a shrunken Charlie Brown than a half-twin.

In the living room, Dina asked Natalie if she wanted to hold him.

"Oh, not yet. He's so tiny," Natalie's mom said.

"She can handle it," Dina said. "What do you think, Natalie?"

"I'll sit on the floor so I don't drop him."

"Good idea," Dina said.

Natalie made a nest with her lap and Dina lowered the baby into it. When Matt began to fuss, Natalie put her finger up to his mouth. Matt sucked on her nail, his weird, no-color eyes crossing.

"You know just what to do," Dina said. "You'll be like a big sister to him. You'll be better than a big sister."

Later, in the kitchen, Dina asked Natalie if she would help her take care of Matt. "I don't know if I can do this on my own," she said.

Natalie didn't like helping out at home: clearing the table, weeding the garden, keeping her room clean. But this was a different kind of help. Her aunt hadn't pleaded, bribed, nagged, or demanded the way her mom did. She had asked. Of course Natalie would help. She fetched baby bottles, retrieved dropped toys, pushed swings, wrestled on jackets and shoes, soothed hurts. She and Dina sat on the bench under the trees at the playground and talked, while Matt ran around and shouted and flung sand out of the sandbox.

Matt was twenty-four now, living in Manhattan and working as a production assistant at an independent film company. Natalie worked at a law firm in Midtown; she took her cousin out for lunch sometimes. Though she and Matt were technically of the same generation, Natalie still felt maternal toward him. She was Dina's friend first, then Matt's cousin. It had always been that way. And now she was even more Dina-like. They were both lawyers, with houses in Connecticut, fifteen minutes away from each other. When Natalie was Matt's age, to work in the city and live outside of it seemed ridiculous. Why spend your free hours in the suburbs when the city itself was freedom? But her husband Ian didn't love it the way she did. He'd gone to work for his dad's business in Stamford, and so they'd bought a house close to his office, rather than continue renting in New York.

Now that Ian was comfortably stationed on a street where the trees formed a canopy overhead, the neighbors tucked away inside stone and brick mini-fortresses, the city was hers again, if only in a piecemeal way. She had the twelve-block walk to and from the train station to her office. She had the view of the Chrysler Building and Bryant Park from the conference room window. She had her lunch hour. She had the occasional night out with friends after work. The commute was its own daily pleasure, arriving in Grand Central Terminal in the morning and returning to it in the evening.

Gazing up at the dreamy green ceiling with its gold-etched constellations was like falling into the sky, if the sky, instead of being changeable and fathomless, was something over which human beings had achieved a triumphant mastery.

Just after Labor Day, Natalie stood in Grand Central and answered a call from her mother. It was six o'clock and the high windows still pitched out bands of light. With the train not due to leave for fourteen minutes, she was in the serene position of watching others scurry.

"You're on your way home?" It sounded like her mother was trying not to cry.

"I have a few minutes. What's going on?"

"I can't discuss it. Not on the phone. Come by later."

"Tell me. I'll worry all the way home. "

"You should worry."

It wasn't what Natalie's mind had leapt to: something had happened to her dad at work, to her grandfather in the nursing home. It was worse than that. Dina, stomach cancer, stage 4.

With its columns and arches, its marble floors and domed ceiling, Grand Central Terminal had a way of drawing everything into itself. Standing there, surrounded by so many sources of light—windows and wall sconces, display boards and information windows, chandeliers and illuminated clocks—one could pretend that grandeur was all. Forget other people. Forget the mind's tedious habits. Forget time. Except that time was master here; you couldn't outwit it. Natalie's train would depart in thirteen minutes, and even if she willfully missed it, another train would arrive in thirty-seven minutes, and another one fifty minutes after that, and then another one, all going to the same place.

TWO PINK LINES YOU WERE pregnant, one pink line you weren't. The instructions didn't say how to interpret a second line so faint it barely seemed to constitute a line at all.

"So you're half pregnant," Ian said.

Unlike the bathroom in their old New York apartment, this bathroom provided plenty of room for two people to deliberate before the sink. The box with the second pregnancy test stick could be easily concealed inside the built-in cabinet. In a few days, Natalie could test herself again. She felt sick enough to chalk it up to pregnancy. It would be a handy excuse to employ for the next eight months. People had to give a pregnant woman a break. Menstruating women were unclean, grouchy, depressed, temporarily insane. Pregnant women were glowing, queenly, care-worthy, life-giving.

"We should celebrate," Ian said.

"I'm really not sure that counts as a line."

Ian took her hand and led her to the living room couch. It was an early October evening, the hour between the sunset and the street lamps. Most of the leaves still clung to their branches; a few weeks of daylight savings time remained. The brown microsuede couch faced the glowing trees. Natalie had spent a lot of time here in the past month, angry not at god but at the idea of god: old man, earth mother, skinny suffering dude, rotund lotus sitter. For seven years, she'd attended Hebrew School twice a week at the Beth Davidson Reform Synagogue, and that hokey-liberal Jewish education had taught her that god was a name in a song, a word in a prayer, a character in a story. He could be conjured up at will. He could also be dismissed. From the cozy couch, Natalie raged silently against the foolish billions who believed in things like transcendence and the afterlife. Why couldn't they see? You could never defeat death.

Ian stroked her feet in his lap. "So, if you are, the baby would come in June. That's a good birthday month. The end of school, the beginning of summer."

"It's not a good time right now," Natalie said.

"It's never the perfect time. That's what everyone says."

"You mean it's always something: a new job, a leaky roof, a little cancer in the family." The foot stroking stopped.

"Don't you think this would be a happy thing? Don't you think everyone would be happy for us?"

"Sure they would."

"Then let's be happy for a minute at least."

Natalie knew Ian would make a great dad. He had this purple terrycloth bathrobe that a dad would wear. He liked to speak in funny voices and talk people through doing things they didn't want to do. And she did want to have children with him someday—when her head was clearer, her nerves calmer, her arms wide open and ready to receive.

THE HOSPITAL THAT HAD REMOVED the tumor in Dina's stomach and was now dispensing the cell-crushing poison had a fancy Manhattan address. A few blocks away, a gallery displayed four floors of Expressionist masterpieces, a shop sold Turkish rugs, a restaurant served truffles and filet mignon. Dina's condition was too critical to allow her to go home between chemo treatments; she was stuck here. Wednesday was Natalie's regular night. Her mom, Matt, and Dina's two closest friends each had theirs. This way, Dina could count on a dependable retinue of visitors, a network, a rotating team. And this way, they didn't have to see each other: the healthy, ill-at-ease loved ones clustered around the sick one. They could each come to her on their own terms, like Catholics in a confession booth. Dina's room overlooked an elegant brick building across the street, with gargoyles minding the cornices. When the nurse came to check Dina's vitals, Natalie stood by the window and studied the gargoyles. They were bug-eyed, open-mouthed, hunched over, as if the weight of the building heaved onto their backs. In medieval times, people thought gargoyles had the power to ward off evil spirits. This seemed like the right idea. Fight ghoulishness with ghoulishness; give fear a suitably fearful shape. Natalie wished the hospital itself were filled with gargoyles rather than with soft-focus paintings of flowers and shorelines, posters printed with inspirational quotes, helpful signage.

December now, holiday time. As she walked down the corridors, Natalie glimpsed wreaths, shiny packages, colorful lights, and cancer patients with all of the fat sucked off their bones. In Dina's room, a rusted gold menorah teetered on the radiator. It had belonged to her mother. As children, Natalie and Matt always went to their grandmother's crumbling apartment in Washington Heights for the first night of Hannukah. They ate latkes fried in pans on all four burners of the stove and jelly donuts plucked from a white bakery box. They made their tuneless way through songs about Maccabees and dreidels. They tore open sixteen packages wrapped in *The Jewish Week* and tied with yarn, eight for Natalie and eight for Matt. Though Natalie's mom would suggest they open one present then and bring the rest home to open one each night, her grandmother would say no. They'd do it like the Christians: everything at once, so you felt like you were rich, for an hour or so anyway. Her grandmother had been dead fourteen years, such a long time it wasn't painful to think of her being dead anymore, though Natalie had loved her, and had run out of the house, away from the family gathering after the funeral, because everyone was just eating banana bread and talking about stupid things.

Dina was sitting up in her hospital bed, wearing the wig Natalie had helped her pick out. It was nicer than her real hair, which had been scrub-brush coarse and shot through with graying frizz. The silky wig hung in soft waves to Dina's shoulders. "I used to spend a lot of time trying to make my hair look like this," she'd said to Natalie when she tried it on. "It never worked. I guess this is my chance to have the hair I always wanted."

Natalie produced a blue box of Hannukah candles from her briefcase and handed it to Dina. "You got the good ones," Dina said. "That sweet Israeli family on the back." A woman with a saintly glow was lighting a giant menorah, while two beautiful boys appeared entranced by their mother's magic. The Western Wall gleamed gold behind them.

Dina opened the box and fingered the wicks. "Do you know why lighting candles is considered a woman's job? Because a woman was responsible for dimming the world's light."

"Jesus. Maybe we should refuse to light them. Is there some male orderly we can call in?"

"Nope. It's all women on this floor at night. Female nurses. Male doctors. You have to wait until morning for your doctor man to breeze through."

Tonight Natalie was supposed to tell Dina that she was pregnant. The first trimester had passed, and Ian had called his parents, his brother, and his best friends with the news. From the couch, Natalie listened to him in the kitchen, where he was preparing a healthy, protein-rich meal, as he'd taken it upon himself to do these days.

In the reverential tone of the pregnancy magazines in the obstetrician's waiting room, he reported on Natalie's morning sickness, the prenatal tests they had scheduled, the delivery options they'd discussed.

They told her parents at Sunday brunch, which Natalie wasn't eating, because omelettes smelled like unborn chicks. Her mom squealed, teared up, rushed about making Natalie a made-to-order breakfast. Her dad said he would build the baby a crib.

"Let me tell Dina," Natalie said.

"Of course," her mother said sharply, acting offended at the suggestion that she might spill the beans. Natalie spent the next week wishing she would.

Natalie had put off telling Dina about other important life events, too: her decision to go to law school, her engagement to Ian. It wasn't that Natalie thought her aunt would disapprove. Dina liked being a lawyer herself; she liked Ian. But Natalie was wary of her own good news, of the way one decision shut down the possibility of another. Dina, more than anyone else she was close to, seemed in some unspoken way to feel that too.

Natalie lit the *shamas*, the servant candle, which was used to ignite the other candles on the menorah. Over the course of eight nights, the *shamas* lit one more candle than it had the night before. Tonight was the first night: two flames. "Let's turn out the light," Dina said, and the two of them sat in the almost dark, with the sounds of creaky carts and cheery nurses.

"I want to tell you something but I'm nervous," Natalie said.

"Okay," Dina said.

"It's silly that I'm nervous." Her mom would have said *Don't be*. Dina would not say that.

"I'm going to have a baby."

"That's wonderful." Natalie could feel Dina looking at her carefully, and she couldn't look back.

"I don't feel that," she said. She was embarrassed to be crying. It was the first time she could remember crying in front of Dina since she was a little girl. She hadn't cried in her presence this entire fall. The doctors had said that even with aggressive chemo, the odds weren't good. The odds of living. That was understood. And Natalie was crying over something else, over something that was supposed to be wonderful.

"I didn't feel it," Dina said. She pulled a tissue from the box on her bedside table and handed it to Natalie. "Not till Matt was more than a month old. I was sick the whole pregnancy. I wanted the baby out of me, but I wasn't ready for him. After he was born, the little sleep I got, I had these nightmares. Somehow we'd left him alone in the house. We were neglectful, or maybe we were dead. Here was my son, completely alone, with no idea what was happening. I could feel his terror as if it were my own. It was, of course."

Dina's voice was Dina's voice, thoughtful and calm. "What was scaring you so much?" Natalie asked.

"You know, in the beginning, there's crying and not crying. There's distressed and there's neutral. I guess I couldn't deal with the lack of positive feedback. I remember when I first felt we had something that might be mutual. Matt was lying in his bassinet, about six weeks old. Suddenly I wanted to sing to him. You know I can't sing. Even 'Happy Birthday'—I move my mouth, but I don't let the sound come out. Man, that day, I sang all the songs I can't sing. 'Whole Lotta Love.' 'Very Young.' 'Heart of Gold.' Matt started making this amazing surprised sound: *Oh, oh, oh*. He was six weeks old, and he liked my singing. I'd been waiting my entire life for someone to want to hear me sing."

It was getting late. They were through with talking. But Natalie didn't want to leave Dina's hospital room until the candles had melted all the way down. One Hannukah night, years ago, Natalie and her mom had to make a semi-emergency trip to the drugstore. As they prepared to leave an empty house behind, the candles in the menorah stood at half their original size, the flames still going strong. Herding Natalie out the door, her mom blew out the candles. By then, age ten or so, Natalie had already considered the existence of god and found him absent from the heavens, but to extinguish the Hannukah candles rather than letting them burn down naturally felt like a great sacrilege. And yet her mother seemed to do it without a second thought.

Complaining of itchiness, Dina removed the wig. She was completely bald. The muscles in her neck bulged; her face was in retreat. Natalie was relieved to have told Dina about the pregnancy. She was't worried anymore that her body was about to betray her. But Dina's body was betraying her at every moment.

NATALIE'S SOPHOMORE YEAR IN HIGH school there was another kind of betrayal, a beginning for Natalie, an ending for Dina. One morning at breakfast, her dad mentioned the new casual Fridays policy at work. He looked good, wearing a pair of khakis and a soft blue shirt that matched his eyes, instead of the usual grey suit and white shirt buttoned up to his chin. After he'd left for the office, Natalie changed into a clingy sweater and a jean skirt. She put on mascara and eyeliner and two coats of rose-brown lipstick. Made-up Fridays: it was worth a shot.

When the bell rang at the end of English class, her crush since fifth grade turned around and asked her out. He used to be Billy. Now he went by William. In middle school he teased her for getting good grades. Now he wanted to hear her thoughts on *The Odyssey*. She spent the rest of the day in a white heat underneath the clingy sweater. Instead of taking the bus, she walked home from school: an hour's trudge through winding streets with old stone houses and scarlet foliage. Her surroundings registered vaguely as beautiful and boring. She was caught up in a meandering fantasy, not about her impending date with William: sitting next to each other in the movie theater, his hand grabbing hers in the dark. There was excitement in that, but it wasn't the real excitement to come, the excitement that the first date of her life would set into motion. She was imagining being older and living in New York City, shimmying down Fifth Avenue on a snowy evening, her long wool coat brushing against the long wool coat of some man, not William, not anyone from Chesterbrook High, no matter how cute he was. They would climb the stairs up to the roof of an apartment building and stand there embracing, pressing all of their heat into each other, while thousands of lights glowing softly in the snow kept promising: more, more, more.

When she arrived home, her mom was on the upstairs phone, shouting about some bastard, some unbelievable bullshit artist. It took Natalie a minute to realize she was talking about Uncle Rob. He'd been having an affair with some woman, cheating on Dina. The kitchen stewed in a mid-dinner preparation mess: chicken breasts half-breaded, boiling potatoes popping out of their red skins, a cutting board full of green beans not yet severed from their pointy ends. Natalie turned off the potatoes and stood by the sink, sneaking slivered almonds. Was it unbelievable that Rob had turned out to be a bastard and a bullshit artist? He was her uncle. He lived a short car ride away, and she had known him all her life. But since she'd developed breasts, he shook hands instead of hugging her. He asked about her grades, and when she started mumbling about A's and A-'s, he boomed, "Excellent, excellent. Keep it up." He was good-looking, with the dentist's requisite gleaming smile and the lean physique of a former college tennis player. He was better looking, more energetic and jovial than Dina, with her serious eyes, her refusal to smile when she didn't feel like smiling. Natalie knew that most people would consider him the better catch. If she thought of him as a man, rather than as her uncle, the truth was she had never much liked him.

When her mom finally came downstairs, she went straight to the refrigerator and pulled out a beer.

"I guess you heard," she said, grimacing, as she popped off the top.

"What's Dina going to do?"

"Smart lawyer—she's already had the divorce papers drawn up."

"How did she find out?"

"Oh, these things leave a trail." Natalie wasn't sure if that meant her mom didn't want to disclose the details, or if she wasn't clear on them herself.

"Does Matt know?"

"They'll tell him tomorrow afternoon, poor boy. What a father. It goes without saying, no New York trip this weekend. You and Daddy and I can go to the movies."

Every other Saturday, some familial combination of Newbergs and Goldmans took the train to Grand Central. From there they went to a museum, or a show, or a street festival, or just out for Chinese food at Ollie's, followed by a long walk. When William had asked Natalie out for this Saturday, she timidly proposed the following

Saturday instead. She could have skipped the family outing, but not without making a bigger deal of this date than she'd felt prepared to do on a day's notice.

"What other questions do you have, Honey? I know this is so hard to process."

After the phone tirade, her mom's good mother persona was kicking into gear, that tone of exaggerated sympathy that never made Natalie want to confess to anything. She wanted to hear about the situation from Dina herself, but she was also afraid to hear it. She had seen her mother hurt many times: crying, shrieking, bearing a crumpled look that made Natalie ashamed for her, rather than compassionate. Though she'd heard Dina speak harshly at times—to Rob, to Matt, to someone at work who was driving her crazy—it was a kind of controlled anger that seemed warranted, even admirable. Natalie didn't want to find her aunt transformed into a pitiable creature, a cheated-upon wife, whether raging or weeping.

"I'll help you finish making dinner," Natalie said, snapping the ends off the green beans.

On Saturday afternoon she sat between her parents at the local movie theater, watching a documentary about the migratory patterns of birds. It was a compromise. Her mom wanted to see a Holocaust drama. Her dad wanted to see a Sci Fi thriller. Natalie wanted to stay home and lie in bed, maybe read *The Odyssey*. The birds on the screen rose up in flocks, circled the skies, voyaged heroically to distant lands. There weren't any people in this movie, just birds: goofy and elegant, striking and plain. To see them going about their lives was a kind of relief.

The next day Dina called and asked Natalie to come over. Rob had taken Matt out for pizza and bowling. Natalie and her aunt sat on the couch eating donuts and watching the wind round up the autumn leaves outside. Dina looked the same as she always looked on a Saturday: her angular frame softer in comfort clothes rather than lawyer clothes, her hair fanned out in a frizzy ponytail, her face sleepy and kinder without makeup. You couldn't tell what had happened by looking at her. Somehow, Natalie had imagined that you could.

Dina asked about the history paper due next week, the debate club Natalie had recently joined. Then she said, "We should talk about what's going on."

"Okay," Natalie said.

"I'm really angry and I'm really hurt. But I'm alright."

"I know." Natalie couldn't think of what else to say.

"Cheating on a spouse is more common than anyone wants to think. Almost half of married couples get divorced. I feel awful, but I'm not special. Do you know what I mean?"

"I think so."

"Some milk would go well with these donuts, wouldn't it?" Dina went into the kitchen and came back with two glasses. She sat back down on the couch and redid her ponytail.

"I'll be a single mother now. I've always thought that would be the hardest thing."

"I'll help you. I'll babysit more. I mean, if you want me to."

"Thanks." Dina sighed. "People expect me to fall apart. They expect me to rail about what pigs men are, to break down in public, this pathetic woman, this poor mother, this tough lady lawyer—look at her now. I won't do it. Do you understand?"

"Yes," Natalie said. She wasn't sure that she did, but whatever Dina wanted her to understand, she wanted to understand it too.

Just before Natalie's mom came to pick her up, Dina suggested that next Saturday she and Matt and Natalie could go to New York, maybe stand on the half-price ticket line and get tickets to a show. Natalie hesitated. She hadn't planned to mention William, felt ashamed to, especially now, but she couldn't not tell her aunt.

"I'm supposed to hang out with this guy next Saturday."

"You are?"

"He asked me yesterday. But we could go another time."

"No, no." Dina smiled. "Come here."

She gave Natalie a hug. Dina's hug was like no one else's. It wasn't the kind of hug you could just lean in for and shimmy back out of. Dina gripped you so hard you had to remember to breathe, had to remember that your body existed alone in space almost all of the time.

"Dating," she said. "I'll have to do it again, I guess. You'll have to tell me what to do."

Since then, seventeen years ago, she'd had many dates, a few of the relationships lasting for a year or more. Rob got married to a hygienist and had another son. But Dina had never married or lived with anyone again. The weekend before the test results came back showing Stage 4 stomach cancer, she'd gone on a first date with a man she'd liked instantly. While she was prepping for surgery, he called and left a message asking her out again. She didn't call him back.

"I've never blown someone off like that," she told Natalie during the first round of chemo. "I feel bad about it. But what could I say? *I'm sorry, I'm having cancer right now. Come see me in the hospital.*"

"You could still call him," Natalie said.

What if—as in one of those romantic cancer movies—Dina had a real chance at love now, sick as she was? Maybe this man would cling to her bedside, worship the beautiful soul beneath the failing body.

"No," Dina said. "No one wants that."

THE HEARTBEAT, CALLED UP FROM its inaudible realm, filled the room with a whumping sound. Outside, it was February, the kind of record-breaking winter that provided a steady source of material for conversations with people in waiting rooms. So cold, so much snow, so many days without sun. The baby would be born in a kinder season.

"140 beats per minute," the technician said. "That's perfectly fine."

A fetal ultrasound was perhaps the only medical procedure that might be seen as joyful, though of course it could reveal terrible news too. But things seemed to be going well. The fetus was projected on the screen, its organs and appendages announced and praised.

"You said you want to know the sex, right?" the technician asked.

"Yes," Natalie said. Ian took her hand. He'd told her he didn't have a preference. She was hoping for a girl, not because of the so-called mother/daughter bond, or because she liked girly things, but because as a girl herself she'd imagined having a girl one day, and it meant something to have that wish fulfilled.

The technician zoomed in on an area, rendering it inscrutable to Natalie. After the birth, they would never want to see inside in this way again. The kid should be all smooth skin and ruffled hair, baby-plump flesh and solid limbs. Never the white bones, the pulsing organs. Never the body beneath its protective layer.

"Definitely a girl," the technician said. "See those three dots? Those are the female genitals." Natalie nodded, though she hadn't really seen them.

"We'll get pictures of this?" Ian asked.

"The radiologist will bring them in. She'll look over the results, but I don't anticipate anything out of the ordinary. Congratulations."

The technician handed Natalie a paper towel to wipe the goop off her belly and left to find the radiologist. It was pleasantly warm and cave-like in the room, the light a muted purple, as if a nearby lava lamp was oozing out blobs of wax.

"A girl," Ian said. "Her features looked kind of feminine, don't you think?"

"Sure," Natalie said.

"Dahlia, then?"

"Dahlia."

They hadn't decided on a boy's name. Devin was one idea, Daniel another. The Jewish tradition was to name a child in honor of a relative who had passed away—none of this goyish So-and-So-Junior stuff. A shared first letter would suffice between the namesake and the baby. Natalie wondered what the Orthodox rabbis would say if the relative's death hadn't happened yet. Would they adjust the rule considering the context, sign off on a couple's choice to name a baby after a dying woman, or would they, in their stickler rabbinical way, insist that not taken by God yet was as good as alive?

CRAGGY AND STEEP ON A cliff above the Hudson River, Fort Tryon Park was wilder than Central Park, less cultivated by picknickers and bicyclists. Natalie's mom and Dina had grown up in an apartment a short walk away from the Heather Garden entrance to Fort Tryon. This park had been Dina's escape when she was feeling angry or depressed. She came to see the fortress of trees and the boats inching down the river.

She came to see the Cloisters, the medieval branch of the Metropolitan Museum of Art, built from the imported remains of French abbeys: a museum packed with so many centuries-old treasures, it was impossible to remain stuck in twentieth-century gloom.

She was about to go into a hospice in Connecticut, and Natalie had driven the two of them here first. She unpacked the two lawn chairs from the trunk of Ian's car and set them on the grass near a patch of daffodils. The shiny trees all boasted new leaves. It was the first week of April, stunningly pretty and warm after the crushing winter. The turning of seasons felt oppressive to her now. If this was to be Dina's last spring, better that it had stayed winter. She opened the car door and helped Dina over to the chair. At seven months pregnant, Natalie knew she shouldn't try to bear the weight of another woman, even one as skinny as Dina was now. At seven months pregnant, she would do what she pleased.

From her lawn chair, Dina asked, the way she spoke now, with all of her breath, "How are you feeling? About the birth."

"I don't know. Weird. I told you we're taking a class? Every time the teacher proposes one of her 'journey to birth' exercise, I can't help groaning. Ian gets annoyed with me. And we have silly homework. For next week we have to bring in a song that somehow embodies our vision of the birth experience."

"What will you bring?"

"'Billie Jean,' I think. Just to needle the teacher."

Dina smiled her cracked smile. "I barely remember what it was like with Matt. Such pain. But I wasn't there somehow. Not the best day of my life. Oh well. The birth is just what has to happen."

What had been the best day of Dina's life? Natalie couldn't bring herself to ask that.

"I can think of a song," Dina said. "For my journey, not yours."

For a moment, Natalie had an impossible thought: Dina was going on a trip. But no—she was just being ironic. She was DNR. She planned to be cremated.

"Pink Floyd, 'The Great Gig in the Sky.' You know it, right?"

"It's a beautiful song."

"That male voice, so calm: 'I am not frightened of dying, any time will do. Why should I be frightened of dying?' And then that woman, just wailing. I always wanted her voice."

"I wanted to tell you." Natalie stopped, sunk her head in her hands, forced herself to keep speaking. "We're going to name her Dahlia. Her Hebrew name will be Devorah—for you."

Natalie lifted her head, opened her eyes. Grass, trees, river, people.

"I like that so much," Dina said.

It happened the way Natalie had hoped, if you could hope for such a thing: Dina going quietly, with Matt by her side, a few days before Natalie's due date. Natalie hadn't really wanted to be there at the moment of the death, and yet, when the call came, she felt that she'd missed something it was unforgivable to miss, though she couldn't have done anything. She couldn't have changed anything.

Then the funeral, the week of sitting shiva at her parents' house. When her grandmother had died, Natalie ran away from the guests and their eating, their useless talk. Now she did as the others did, sat in a chair and listened politely.

She was so smart.

What lovely June weather.

She was so independent.

Did you know Arthur is going to France?

She was so strong.

Have some more potato salad.

People hugged her gently and said reasonable things. "I bet you're ready for that baby to pop out already," and "What a shame your aunt didn't get to meet her."

Natalie said, "Yes." She said, "I know." If this world without Dina seemed a fake, why not be nice, why not be agreeable? Why not let Frank get her a pillow to ease her neck, a footstool to rest her legs? Why not smile when Ethel said that having a child was the best thing you could do, the best thing she'd ever done?

At forty-one weeks, Natalie went in to the hospital for a stress test. If she passed it, her doctor was willing to let her keep going for another week. But the nurse came back with the test results; she'd failed. Her amniotic fluid was too low. Natalie hadn't been able to imagine what the pain of labor would be like. Now she didn't have to.

"Tell me when you can't feel any pressure here," the surgeon said, and a minute later, Natalie couldn't feel anything. Ian sat in a chair by her head, the curtain shielding below her waist. He'd been excited to watch the baby being born through her legs. This he didn't want to see. After a while the surgeon said, "Would you like to meet your daughter?"

Looking at Ian's glowing face beneath the surgical cap, Natalie felt as if it were really to him that this inconceivable thing was happening. The doctors pronounced the baby in perfect shape and delivered her to her father. Natalie's arms were shaking too much from the epidural to be of any use. Ian cradled Dahlia, holding her up so that Natalie could see. She looked rosy and peaceful, with dark brown tufts of hair and blue-grey slanted eyes. It wasn't then—touching the tiny hands with trembling fingers, or fitting the pursed lips around her nipple, or seeing her mom weep, her dad kiss Dahlia's forehead—it wasn't until late that night, when Natalie lay in the hospital bed, a patient recovering from abdominal surgery, that she knew she'd been wrong.

Ian was asleep in the armchair by the window. Dahlia was asleep in the bassinet. There they were: her family. She'd been acting as if her whole family was dying, her whole family was gone. It was wrong to have built a scale with her own hands, set Dina on one side, the baby on the other, and then backed away, giving in to gravity. It wasn't her choice to make, but she should have chosen, in that terrible game, to bring her baby before Dina, just for one moment, and let them breathe the same air. Not that it mattered now. There was no god granting her wishes, or punishing her, or trying to teach her a lesson. It was just one death on one June morning, one birth on another. For them, Natalie would sing all the songs she couldn't sing.

MARK HALLIDAY

Drinking with Zoe

So I was fairly depressed in a drab-grime sort of way feeling
all roads lead to silly ego of everybody and grabs for dumb power
and we all say the same stuff about it all, so I told Zoe

but she tilted her head and got that sweet-but-ironic look
and said "Have you read *The Tall Tale of Tommy Twice*
by Nathan Leslie?" and I said no. I drank more pale ale

and tried again to explain that the absurdity of human repetition
becomes ugly—but Zoe nodded and asked me if I had read
An End to All Things by Jared Yates Sexton and I said no,

never heard of it. Zoe smiled in her sly way, but I had so much
to say about human pathos being dreary like a shopping mall
at closing time on a Wednesday in some rainy winter

when nobody cares and all desires are obviously idiotic.
Zoe said "Interesting. Have you read *Fight For Your Long Day*
by Alex Kudera?" I said are you making these up?

Zoe said, "Or what about *The Absent Traveler* by Randall DeVallance?"
I said by who? "Randall DeVallance," Zoe said, so I said
"Oh, right, isn't that a pseudonym for Thomas Pynchon?"

"We may never know," Zoe said. We ordered another pale ale for me
and Scotch for her. I said, "So have you read these weird books?"
"Not yet," she said, "but I plan to live a long time and read

seven hundred messed-up books and maybe two hundred fantastic books
and then go for a long walk in the messed-up metropolis
and sink down on the steps of the library and read a hot scene

in some deeply flawed novel I've checked out and then
check out myself, and just before the book drops from my gnarly grasp
my ancient glittery eyes are gonna be, like, gay."

PAIGE ACKERSON-KIELY

Ellesmere Island

You have a job at a pet store. $9/hour. You face the leashes and dog toys, clean the cages and place the rodents destined for the boa constrictor into the freezer first, because you've read Jack London and know that they will go numb, which will hurt, but then they will go to sleep, which is, in your experience, gentle. There is a heroin epidemic in your small, northern town. People going numb all over the place. You don't know their names, you don't name them. Lake Hazen, on Ellesmere Island, is a thermal oasis. In the summer it gets so warm you can walk in up to your neck. Still, everyone craves the buried heart 1,000 meters deep in the ice. It'll take a bomb to open that baby up, to expose those guts, to get to the thing we all take for granted as alive. You're comforted by Ellesmere Island, where rats might sleep for thousands of years, waiting for scientists to chip them out, to insert the long needle into their necks. A man who lost his shirt in the woods holds up the pet store with a fishing knife. For a moment you are frozen, but then you put the bills on the counter and raise your hands in the air. The beast in the freezer shifts on the rack, closes its eyes. The shirtless man does the same in the parking lot. 120 people visit Lake Hazen every summer and take pictures. During your lunch break you scroll through them on your phone.

MARTHA COLLINS

from Admit One: An American Scrapbook

Better Babies

In 1911, the Iowa State Fair, which was one of the country's
    oldest agricultural and industrial expositions,
which used the same grandstand, some of the same cattle swine
    sheep and poultry barns and pavilions I saw as a child,
which had featured an Indian village, high-diving horses, bicycle
    races, and in 1896 had staged its first locomotive collision—

in 1911, the Fair featured the Wright Brothers, the first of many cows
    made of butter (famous when I was a child and even now),
as well as its first Baby Health Contest, conceived by physician
    Florence Sherbon and P.T.A. leader Mary T. Watts,
who had asked: *You are raising better cattle . . . horses . . . hogs,
    why don't you raise better babies?* And so:

In 1911 babies were measured for height, weight, *anthropometric
    traits and mental development,* and advertised and displayed,
in an automobile in the Fair's Parade, as *Iowa's Best Crop.*

By 1916, when the Fair's lawns were mowed by sheep
    and the first 4-H Club Baby Beef Contest was held,
most states had Better Baby Contests, many co-sponsored
    and advertised by *The Woman's Home Companion,*
which conferred certificates and prizes on winning babies.

In 1911, Charles Davenport published *Heredity in Relation to Eugenics*
    and urged Sherbon and Watts to *score 50% for heredity.*
In 1913 Watts wrote that *Eugenic Expositions*
    were often associated with the contests,
and by 1920 the women had helped Better Babies evolve
    into Fitter Family Contests, also held at state fairs.

Fitter Families

Yea, I have a goodly heritage my mother
said her sister said the Bible said
and it does and they did we do but

that was also the motto of Fitter Families
for Future Firesides, contests featured
at state fairs using anthropometric

measurements medical dental vision
exams intelligence tests evaluations
of personality for families some

with several generations as well
as eugenic family histories. The forms
had a blank for *race* (which could be *Nordic*)

and charts were posted with literacy rates
for NATIVE-BORN FOREIGN-BORN NEGROES
as well as birth rates for NATIVE-BORN ALIEN

There were also displays with flashing lights

This light flashes every 15 seconds
O
Every 15 seconds $100 of your money
goes for the care of persons with bad
heredity such as the insane, feeble-
minded, criminals and other defectives.

—and medals awarded to winners, which read:

YEA, I HAVE A GOODLY HERITAGE

Some Eugenics

Marriage selection / large
families encouraged for the fit

Legal prohibition of marriage
by the unfit: the feeble-minded epileptic
indigent inebriate insane in 30 states by 1914

                    —but the unmarried

Legal segregation of the feeble-minded etc.
in asylums training schools colonies

              —but the expense

Legal sterilization of
in 15 states by 1916

              the prime duty the inescapable duty of the good citizen of the right type
                    is to leave his or her blood behind him. . . . we have no business
                          to permit the perpetuation of citizens of the wrong type.
                    (Theodore Roosevelt to Charles Davenport, 1913)

In 1916, Stanford's Terman revised the Binet-Simon test
which Henry Goddard had translated and used since 1908
and for which he invented the word *moron* (from Greek, *dull*)
for the *feeble-minded*, the *high-grade defectives*.

In 1917, Terman used the test to determine officer fitness
and after the war tested school children, finding mental
deficiency high among Mexicans, Negroes, Italians.

How did the little . . . Why did the little . . .
What did the little moron say . . .

In the 1917 film *The Black Stork*,
Dr. Harry Haiselden—Illinois surgeon
and practitioner of *lethal eugenics*, who had refused
to perform surgery on a number of *defective* newborns—
played a version of himself refusing to save such a child.

what are taken to be divine laws and a sentimental belief in the sanctity of human life tend
to prevent both the elimination of defective infants and the sterilization of such adults as are
. . . of no value to the community. The laws of nature require the obliteration of the unfit.
(Madison Grant)

Fit / Fit

healthy   hearty   worthy   made

to fight   explore   rule   a good

fit for a   fit the facts

to be   fit   as befitting

un-   diseased   defective   dragging

down   might have a   right

here in the yard   to be tied   so can't

have more   of them   select

fit into a   square   a round

of weeping   anger   and starts

to be stopped   before   they throw

a poor   poor   and if the shoe

BRUCE BOND

Circle

So when I arrived in hell, the sign said,
If you lived here, you'd be home by now,
and while I did not get the joke, I read
the language reading me. I knew it knew
great suffering can feel a little homeless,
and then the smell of hair in the distance.
And I followed, the way one life follows
one man and grows long as the sun goes down.
That's me, looking for a chance to call
home and say, I have not abandoned you,
Hope. The prison architecture of hell
is, as comedies go, a nightmare, true.
But dreams open what they close. Like circles.
And we, on fire, are only passing through.

Bosch

If you hear a laugh in the dreary choir
whose punishment for song is song, scored
in blood on the buttocks at the altar,
be kind. Given all the fates we die for,
it's the scatology of torment kids love,
screaming in glee to see the bird-monster
whose mating call is bodies, eaten alive.
To hell, it says, with heaven and its lyres
that break no heart. In a better world,
hurdy gurdies grind people into music,
music into you. Go ask the child.
There is an art to joy like this, a trick,
where the love of God does not love us,
or anyone much. Then, with grace, it does.

MARC PALTRINERI

Life Is Beautiful

I'm not sure I want to be happier
the gray trees the silver fog are
just so beautiful
and lonely I would like to wear them
around feel their weight
maybe stop by say hello
to the powerlines
another beautiful shaved spot on this earth
you can see all the way through the
next town and I know
a little what it's like to be a powerline
and stand branchless
and naked in a field of burnt grasses
I can almost hear them
buzzing up there about me saying
Hello good to see you
We too were lonely and so we came to this place
and maybe this day will seem
not as old as the others
the fog beginning to open
making room for a lightness
coming through
and here's noon she's brought some roses
Oh you shouldn't have I say
You really shouldn't

JULIE MARIE WADE

Doppelgänger

All my students look like Ashley Olsen,
even the boys. I say this not to disparage them.

They are green & newly grown. Their smiles
are too big for their small faces. They shift

their bodies as if on stilts. They wait for the
laugh track before they make their next move.

I feel older now. I think I remember them
as children, child stars.

Didn't we once cross the Golden Gate Bridge together?

How strange to see them here again, assembled,
this new version of *Full House*,

& I the single father of this class of Ashley Olsens
who sometimes, while my back is turned,

arrange themselves into rows of Mary-Kates.

LISA KO

Pat + Sam

1

B<small>EFORE THE PARTY</small> P<small>AT SPENT</small> an hour crying in her bedroom—her and Harry's room, their old room—and used up a stick of concealer trying to hide the crinkled half-moons under her eyes. She left the girls with the neighbors. She put on lipstick. At the party she asked Sam Kwan for a light.

It was a cold October night in 1974. They smoked back then, everybody did. This was before Pat's two children became Sam's and before there were three children, before they grounded the oldest when Pat found a pack of Newports in her room. By then they would have forgotten their own youth, or rather, they would hold their children to higher standards. The children would be confident and happy—they'd feel entitled to happiness—and for that Pat and Sam would resent them.

Pat told Sam she used to live in the city, but now she lived in Jersey. Some friends had invited her to the party, so she'd driven out to her old neighborhood in Queens. "Where I live," she said, "it's like the country, but there's a train to the city."

Sam told Pat he lived in Brooklyn and never went to New Jersey. "It must be nice to have trees and grass."

The apartment was a dump, the room too hot and crowded, the moss-green carpet balding in patches, like a neglected lawn. To the right of the sunken couch was a folding table with a paper plate of pretzel crumbs, a six-pack of beer, and a plastic jug of deli gin.

"What's the guy's name that lives here?" Pat asked in Cantonese.

Sam recognized the words and said, "I have no idea. My friend Ben invited me."

Sam's laugh was a joyful bark, and Pat thought she saw, through his thick eyeglasses, the glint of a troublemaker.

The music surged. Annabelle Uy leapt off the couch and started shaking her hips, rear end plump and wide like a bakery bun. "Dance, Pat, dance," Annabelle shouted, pointing to Pat, and Pat looked at Sam and he shrugged—why not.

Even if she didn't care that much about dancing, Sam's willingness to do so made him more appealing. They danced, not terribly, but not particularly well. Their shoulders remained hunched, feet rooted to the floor. Their arms swung slowly but they moved closer to one another.

The next day Pat's mother called and said, "I don't know how you do it, all alone in that big house with two little children. All alone and nobody to help you. I don't see why you can't move back to Chicago already."

"All right, Ma," Pat said. "I met someone."

"Who?"

"He's Chinese. We're going out next Saturday."

"Oh?"

"He has a good job. And he knows all about the kids and Harry."

"And he's still talking to you? There must be something wrong with him."

"Nothing's wrong with him!"

"But he'll want his own house."

"He likes New Jersey. He thinks it's nice."

Her mother made a pleased, cooing sound.

2

HE HAD NEVER BEEN WITH a woman longer than four months, and that was years ago, in Hong Kong, with a girl named Helen whose voice could peel the skin off babies. Sam was just her type; locked up, quiet-angry, a kid who had lived in ten different homes after his father left and his mother went to find work in Singapore. In Hong Kong he had wanted to be a musician. He put on his one good outfit and went to the Sunday afternoon tea dances when he could afford it, screamed and danced to The Lotus belting out *I'll be waiting I'll be waiting I'll be waiting*, the chorus pressing into him like a thumb against a vein. He could strum a guitar and keep a beat but that's as far as his music dreams went. His high school teachers said engineering was the way to get a student visa, so he put engineering on his application and Nebraska gave him a full scholarship. After four long years in Omaha he boarded a bus for New York, watched the flat fields of the Midwest bump by as if they were unspooling toilet paper, ready to flush down the drain.

New York was a platter of girls: towering blondes with custard tits, smooth-skinned babes with sultry lips. When Sam talked it felt like his words were criss-crossing in the air, scrambled before they landed. Things that sounded fine in his mind left his mouth and entered women's ears in some garbled syntax. "Nice dress," he said, and they looked at him like he'd groped them on the subway. "Buy you a drink?" They'd recoil like he'd spit in theirs.

He went to record stores and jazz clubs and sat alone in the back. What they saw: A scrawny Chinese guy, barely any meat on his bones, five-foot-seven on a good day, Coke-bottle glasses, cheap clothes, an underfed accountant's underfed accountant loser brother. They saw a man who couldn't dance. They heard a man who couldn't sing.

But in his leaky water-balloon heart, Sam could sing and dance. In the apartment he shared with a rotating cast of roommates, he locked the door to his room and played records on his turntable, James Brown and Maceo Parker, Sly Stone. It felt like being unraveled.

I lost someone, my love
Someone who's greater than the stars above
I wanna hear you scream!

He hadn't lost a love like that. His father—that was a loss, but not of a real person, only the idea of father. Yet there was always a feeling of incompleteness, a reaching for, a wanting of. Some thread left unstitched. The missing chunk. Late at night in his room, he dreamt of meeting a woman who would understand all of that, who'd be able to listen to music and feel the notes crawl up her spine, who would sing along, who would dance with him, who would leave him alone.

His buddy Ben lived with a girl named Lily in a studio apartment in Chinatown that smelled like overcooked eggs, both of them skinny enough that they'd sometimes share clothes. The idea of living with a girl seemed as improbable to Sam as waking up on the moon. Shacking up, Ben called it. He cheated on Lily with a college girl who wore matching dresses, shoes, and panties and a rich jook-sing with a Pomeranian that slept in her bed and woke him up by licking his toes. "We're too young to be tied down," Ben told Sam, and Sam pictured himself splayed out on his back, limbs spread, hands and feet tied snugly to four posts in the ground, Helen from Hong Kong triple knotting the ropes.

Pat was a woman with very little curve to her, smooth hips and flat ass, dark hair permed into a frizzy halo. Behind rounded red frames, her eyes were wet and giant, her nose and mouth miniature. She had the look of a doll owl. Doll owl, Sam thought, turning the words around in his mouth.

"Fire me up." Those were the first words she said to him, the sentence he would later see as the spark; or, on worse days, the culprit.

She wanted a light—she wanted to be *fired up*.

3

ON THE NIGHT OF HER and Sam's first official date, Pat had already spoken on the phone to her mother and Annabelle Uy.

"Make sure you look good for once," her mother said. "It wouldn't kill you to put on a little make-up and wear a dress. Wear heels because you're such a little shrimp.

But not too-high heels. Remember, you don't want to be taller than the man. You haven't gained any weight, have you?"

Annabelle said, "I asked Jack Ng who asked Ben Chan who said that Sam was quiet but a stand-up guy. But really? You gotta watch out for those quiet ones. He must like you if he's going all the way out to New Jersey. Watch out!"

Pat was dressed in red slacks and a cream-colored, V-neck blouse, curls sprayed tight, mascara and eyeliner carefully applied. Sam was arriving on the six o'clock train. Lynette and Cynthia were wearing corduroys and turtlenecks, hair pulled into long pigtails. The Mulligans up the block were out of town, the Antonicellis already had plans for the night, and Pat didn't know anyone else in Warwick, so she told the girls they were going out for dinner with a friend.

When Sam asked her out she thought they could see each other just this one time, and then she'd never have to tell him about Harry and the girls.

"Can we have pizza?" Cynthia asked.

"We'll see," said Pat. "Behave yourselves, we're the guests."

At Romeo's they got looks. The barn-shaped pizzeria was noisy, the air heavy with grease. There were a few empty tables but the waitress told Sam and Pat to wait, and they stood in a small corner space by the door, the girls droopy and shivering with their backs pressed against a cigarette machine. Each time the door opened, it brought in more cold air. Family after family came in, spoke to the waitress, waited until their names were called, and sat down. Sam and Pat watched as those families flipped through menus and placed orders. When the waitress brought out a pepperoni pie and a pitcher of soda, Cynthia tugged at Pat's coat and said, "Why aren't we eating yet?"

Twenty minutes had passed and her stomach was growling. Sam's face was creased and tight. He shook his head and pushed his way to the waitress. "Why are we still waiting?" He pointed to Cynthia and Lynnette. "Children are waiting." It sounded like he was shouting.

The waitress had a nose like a soft banana, a small pouch of fat under her otherwise thin face. She was taller than Sam, and as he shouted at her, she took a step back.

"We haven't been seated. You seated those families first, and they came in after us." Sam pointed to the family eating the pepperoni pie, then back at the waitress, jabbing a finger.

The waitress looked at him as if he was in speaking another language. "Pardon me?"

Pat wanted Sam to punch the waitress. She wanted to punch the waitress herself. Sam stood there, glaring, his hands shoved into his coat pockets.

"Say something," Pat whispered.

Sam said nothing. She felt relieved that he didn't make a scene. How would she have explained it to the girls? Maybe they had imagined everything, maybe there really weren't any tables available, maybe all the families that came in after them were close relatives of the waitress and they were just being paranoid.

"Let's go," Sam said. It was a command, a bark. Without looking back, he kicked the door open and walked out. Pat waited to see if he'd return or open the door for her, but he didn't. She took the girls' hands and pushed the door open herself.

Sam stood in the parking lot with his fists balled. "Those fuckers."

"Don't yell. You're scaring the girls."

"They think they can walk all over us!"

Pat took out her car keys and wondered if she could ever return to Romeo's. "They're not all that bad."

He took out a pack of cigarettes. "Want one?"

"I don't smoke around the girls."

Sam put the pack back into his pocket. The girls climbed into the backseat and stared at him. Pat wanted to give them a hug.

Cynthia said, "I'm hungry."

4

TREES WERE DIFFERENT IN NEW Jersey, bigger, more colorful. The train had rolled past houses with single-car garages, three-block downtowns, stores with awnings, even an official town clock. Pat had said on the phone to look out for the green Beetle, and he spotted it when he got off in Warwick, the only car in the lonely parking lot with its lights on. Two little girls sat in the backseat, watching him.

"These are my daughters. Lynette and Cynthia. Say hello to Sam."

"Hello," the children chorused.

Sam's brain was flipping through the possibilities. Who were these children? Was this a set-up? Pat didn't wear a wedding ring; she had agreed to the date. Should he get out of the car before her husband returned and kicked his ass all the way back to Brooklyn?

She put her hand on top of his. It was small and warm, clammy with sweat.

"I'm sorry I didn't say anything earlier. I didn't know how. My husband, Harry, well, my ex-husband, he passed away."

"I'm so sorry."

The girls were silent.

"It was almost a year ago."

Only? Almost? "I'm sorry."

Pat clapped her hands together and turned on the ignition. "I couldn't get a sitter for tonight," she said in Cantonese.

Sam looked at her, then towards the back seat.

"They don't understand," Pat said. "Their father was jook-sing, Chinese but born in America."

"Oh?"

"We met in Queens."

"Oh."

"Are we going for pizza?" one of girls asked. "Do you like pizza?"

"I love pizza," Sam said, switching back to English, even though eating cheese gave him stomach cramps.

At Romeo's he wished they were in the city, where there were other Chinese, and later he would feel that he had backed down too easily, that he should've gone back inside and let the waitress know they couldn't mess with him. He wondered if, in not doing so, he had let Pat down.

Pat drove them to another pizzeria and they ordered a pie to go, brought it back to the house, and ate it at the kitchen table. The girls drank sodas, Pat and Sam beers. The scene at Romeo's receded, somewhat. Sam was surprised at how large the house was on the inside. The ceilings were tall, and the fluffy shag carpet clean and warm. The kitchen was twice the size of his rented room, and the windows faced a tree-filled back yard. He walked around the living room full of hanging plants and children's toys and looked at framed photos on the fireplace mantle. The jook-sing husband was in some of them, and Sam noted that he wasn't too tall, although he was good-looking, with hard, chiseled features and wiry hair. The girls took after him.

There was a picture of Pat and the jook-sing husband smiling in front of a small Christmas tree strung with so much tinsel it was if the tree had metallic hair. They wore matching red plaid pants. Had this been the jook-sing husband's last Christmas? He didn't look sick. Sam looked at his deceased competition—for now he had put himself into the running—and Pat began to take on a new shape, that of a steely, vulnerable survivor. Someone who'd been wanted, before.

Then she was standing next to him. "I'm sorry," she said. "This isn't much of a date."

Sam wanted to scoop her into his chest. "It's okay." He reached over and put an arm around her shoulders, patting her at regular intervals.

"His name was Harry," she said, "and he died in a car accident."

5

SAM WASHED THE DISHES AS Pat put the girls to bed. In the bathroom mirror, dark circles beneath her eyes were emerging like storm clouds, and she decided he had only asked her out because he was being kind. She brushed her tongue with her toothbrush to scrub off the cheese taste and walked downstairs. She would drop Sam off at the train station and go to sleep and wake up at six-thirty, get the girls off to Warwick Elementary and get herself to the lawyers' office on Route 17 where she worked as a paralegal—two exits south of where Harry had died—and pick the girls up from school, fix dinner, mediate when Cynthia pinched Lynette and Lynette cried, plant them in front of the television, hug them when they said they missed Daddy, and fall asleep in her work clothes at nine o'clock. She would think again about selling the house and moving back to Queens.

The kitchen was empty and the back door open. Sam was in the middle of the yard, looking at the sky. The shadows lent him solidity. His zip-up jacket was old and cheap looking but it gave him the appearance of heft. For a moment she wondered who this man was and what he was doing in her yard. Pat walked towards him, the leaves damp beneath her boots. She would have to rake them; she had never raked leaves in her life.

"I'm smelling the sky," he said. "It smells good, the fresh air."

"Maybe you're not a city type after all. Maybe you belong in New Jersey."

"Maybe," he said, and as they studied each other through their glasses he leaned down an inch, she up an inch, and they made out like teenagers. He felt less flimsy than he looked, his hands gripping her waist, and when her mouth opened and closed she was surprised by how promptly she was turned on, how acutely she wanted more.

6

WHEN YOU START TO HOPE, then comes the danger. You begin to think that love is like song lyrics, and then you're in trouble.

He listened to too much music and he wanted too much—a deep gnawing, a terrible hunger, an uppercut to the heart. He pictured himself standing at Pat's doorway holding flowers in one hand and a bundle of records in the other. They could save one another from all the lonely days after lonely days.

He went to work at the drafting job he hated, marked up the Help Wanted ads, and slept fitfully in his room, thinking of dark backyards and big trees. In Pat's backyard he had seen stars, shining so hard it was as if they were vibrating, quivering from the effort of producing all that light.

Riding the subway into Manhattan, Sam imagined being a father. He had no idea how to deal with children, never mind girls, the girls of the woman he was dating and a dead man. Walking through Midtown, he wondered if he was ready for the challenge—was he being challenged?—and his walk grew faster and stronger. Hadn't he traveled across the world by himself? If the jook-sing husband could be a father, he could. In New Jersey there were no Chinese but the air was so clean. Not like Omaha, where open space was like strangling.

They fell into a routine. Pat picked him up at the train station on Sundays. Sam brought Lynette and Cynthia coloring books and asked them questions about their favorite TV shows. Pat told him about the accident and Sam said nothing because it scared him. He was simply listening to her, being supportive. He wondered if he could be satisfied being her second choice, if the jook-sing husband would have gone back inside the pizzeria, yet sometimes he thought that being second was better than not being a choice at all.

It would be easier if she didn't have kids.

Pat had yet to visit him in Brooklyn, and he didn't want to ask her, knowing it would be hard with the girls. But he wanted her to spend the night with him, to prove she was interested.

"I think you should come stay with me one night," he said, after almost two months of Sunday visits. "I really think you need to."

7

"So, DID YOU MAKE IT with him yet?"

"What? Annabelle!"

"Did you, or didn't you?"

"No!" Then Pat added, "Not yet."

"Come on," said Annabelle. "There's no need to play the prude."

"He's come by six Sundays in a row," Pat said.

Annabelle laughed. "Now it's serious."

Pat thought of the way her heart beat after she and Sam made out in the yard each Sunday, how they took their glasses off and looked at each other as if they were seeing new people. He looked bare, slippery, different.

"Maybe I'm falling in love?" she said.

Annabelle screeched and dropped the phone.

Her mother called and said, "Don't push him away. You can't be so picky at your age."

Contrary to what her mother thought, Pat was still young, but she didn't feel young. Still, Sam would be content with not knowing all the details that came before him. He wouldn't ask.

He was still coming into focus for her. The lens would adjust, and on some days she would see him shaped into the same type of man as Harry, slim hips and swagger, all muscle, ready to fire. Harry and Pat had worked next door to one another in Queens. He did taxes. She did filing. It seemed like before she knew it, she had married him, given birth to two children, and moved out to New Jersey, envisioning life as a whimsical crapshoot, a leisurely canoe ride down a river on an endless summer afternoon, floating on a current that would take her wherever it pleased. She played along, believing that she didn't have much of a choice, but she had chose Harry, she had chose him hard. There had been boyfriends before, mild-mannered boys that Pat neither loved nor hated. But they had judged her passiveness to be disinterest and eventually backed away. Only Harry had seen it for what it was. An invitation. A cracked door.

She used to try to catch Harry in unguarded moments, look at him across the room as he ironed shirts in his boxer shorts, had to sit on her hands to stop herself from pushing herself into him. He had made her feel crazy and out of control, as if she'd wanted him until there was no want left in her.

Whoever came next would get the crumbs.

On other days, the lens would adjust and Sam's shape would recede, the lines of his body redrawn into another man, the illusion of cockiness fine-tuned into a shape Pat couldn't yet read.

The first time he saw her car in the daylight he asked her about the dent in the fender. She explained that it was a new car, the old one had been wrecked in the accident. The dented fender was from Pat's own accident.

"After he died I was so scared I couldn't drive on the highway. Then one day I took the car out and drove it into the pond in Warwick."

"Why?" he asked.

"I don't know. Maybe because he died, I was safe. Superstitious, you know?"

They were sitting at the kitchen table, their feet rubbing against one another. Pat put her hand against her mouth. Her breath wet her palm. She wanted to rewind and snatch back everything she'd just revealed.

Sam looked at her with confusion and pity. The minutes ticked by and he said nothing. He said nothing.

Pat removed her feet from his. Finally, he said, "Then what happened?"

"The car was a little banged up, but I wasn't hurt. I told everyone it was an accident, and they believed me." He put his arm around her and she felt so relieved she said, "I can get a sitter for next weekend."

At dinner in Manhattan Chinatown, Pat ate quickly and greedily. Afterwards, as they walked to Sam's apartment, she felt like a schoolgirl swinging hands with her boy. She belonged here! She was in love! She was so lucky to feel this way twice!

Don't be too proud, her mother used to tell her. A little proud is okay. Too much is not okay.

All Pat wanted was a less busy heart.

In Sam's apartment the floorboards slanted dramatically to the right, and the tiny living room held only a television set on a plastic crate and several plastic chairs. She imagined picking up his dirty beer bottles and dishes every night after work. His room was similarly small and bare, a twin mattress lying resigned in the corner, the floor coated in so much dirt that Pat was afraid to take off her shoes.

They sat on the mattress and kissed. Sam's mouth tasted like dinner. They kissed for a long time.

He got up and pulled a record from a stack of albums in the corner, placed it on the turntable that sat on an overturned cardboard box, and gently lowered the needle. The music began. It was strange music, some song she'd never heard before. It sounded like a man yelping, screaming words about losing someone.

"What do you think? Do you like it?" Sam's glasses were off, his face expectant.

"I don't know," Pat said. "It's so loud. So much screaming."

He looked disappointed, so she said, "Okay, then let's dance." They got up and danced in the space between the mattress and the wall. Pat giggled at how silly the scene was, the loud music, the sad room. Sam didn't laugh back. His face was still and serious.

No humor.

What was so serious about this shrieking music, anyway?

What was the big deal?

8

IT WAS TIME TO DO it. It was over too soon. He was embarrassed.

She didn't understand his music. She hated his apartment. He'd seen the way her mouth pinched when she saw his room.

He hated her for that, and he hated himself for caring that the jook-sing husband had been able to buy her that huge house. Pat acted like she was too good for the city.

"Sam?"

She lay beside him, naked. He pulled the sheets over her, not wanting to see the paunch on her stomach, the floppy, ridiculous skin.

"Sam?" Pat asked again. He felt like he was being drowned. "Do you have a cigarette? Sam?"

Sam thought he was too young to be tied down, but that morning Ben had called from a pay phone in Lake Tahoe, where he was on a skiing trip. "We're moving to California," Ben announced. "I asked Lily to marry me and she said yes."

Ben said it was time to make his real life start, and Sam said he hadn't realized that what he'd been living wasn't real life. When he put the phone down he realized that his early days in New York were over.

PAT EXHALED SMOKE. THE RECORD player spun static. Sam was quiet, his hair sticking up in a cowlick. He curled away from her, breathing. Was he sleeping or only pretending to?

"You know, women sometimes take longer."

She said it and knew she shouldn't have. It was only their first time. It could get better. She said his name again, and he said nothing.

Outside, it was dark already. Pat heard a bus screech on the street, footsteps and voices in the next room. Four roommates, all single men. She had to use the bathroom, but she was trapped here until the roommates left.

The room was cold and she missed her girls. There were nights, alone with them in the house, that she thought she could do this life solo. It wasn't so bad, just the three of them. On other nights, she felt like she was the only person left in the world, with two girls and a dead husband and nowhere to go, and she was so angry she wanted to smash the walls with an ax, throw chairs through the windows.

She dragged deeper on the cigarette, trying to outrun the sinking feeling. Her mother had said, "I'm so happy, I'm so relieved. I'm so happy you met a nice man."

"Are you awake?" Pat asked now, in a last effort, and Sam didn't respond. The space between them, imperceptible at first, became a sudden tear, threads popping from seams in one sure stroke.

But he was nice enough, she thought. He was a nice man.

JAMES RICHARDSON

Vectors 4.3: A Summer Morning

Like a word I've looked up and forgotten.

•

After the shower there's a dry shadow under the maple. Even in this suburban wood there are square inches no one has stepped in since the beginning of time. I bet there are very small spaces time itself has missed.

•

I'm so slow to speak that even silence puts words in my mouth.

•

What was our original sin—disobedience? dishonesty? sex? self-consciousness? The story doesn't care, as long as we remember the part about having to labor to make up for it.

•

I'm not really doing nothing. I'm working hard not to get in the way of whatever should be doing itself.

•

In their changeless Eden, Adam and Eve could only be tempted by the need to be in a story.

•

A tiny pain is like a light in the woods. Hard not to go find out what it is.

•

Under *boredom* my dictionary says *origin unknown*.

·

Gods don't read.

·

Sin derives from *es*, the *It is* in a formula something like *It is (true); I did it*. But confession is more than admitting guilt: otherwise, you could just confess to yourself. It is giving up the hope that what you did was uniquely yours, and maybe, just maybe, excusable. What you did is a story others will think they've heard before. What you're admitting is that they're right.

·

I guess that was my choice, though what I really wanted was not to choose at all.

·

They revised the Lord's Prayer to *Forgive us our debts as we forgive our debtors*: since we have to believe in what we owe if we want to believe we have something coming to us.

·

You offer help, and suddenly it's more complicated: I have to decide to really do it, and to trouble you, and to owe you.

·

To be late is to say my time is worth more than yours; to be early, the opposite. But time changes from precious to worthless and back again in no time at all, and we have no idea what we're taking from each other.

·

We say *I have no time*, we hear *I have no time for you*.

·

Left to itself, Time stops, maybe an hour a day—who knows, since you're by definition unaware. Otherwise, it's propelled by crossing things off lists, putting away dollars, tucking vista after vista into tiny cameras. Even as you dispose of one thing, another rushes in to fill the void, and the little wind it makes is Time. In his last years, my father had a tape deck, a video camera and four VCR's running. Probably he was recording more hours than he actually lived, a Saint of Time, doing it all for the rest of us, bringing on the end.

•

The moment was mine, until I tried to give it to you. Or to keep it for myself, which is the same thing.

•

The moralists told us the vice of age was avarice, but what I saw in my great teachers 20 years later was bitterness that they had not been recognized for what they had done. By now, I feel how deeply *to have* and *to have done* are the same. The resumé is another kind of bank account, and harder to let go of. *Sell all you have*, said a better teacher than any of us.

•

Sad that what's good for the ego is seldom good for the soul.

•

My father, a Depression child, never quite believed in Money. *If you like it, buy two* was his motto, and he turned his salary into Things, their backups, and the tools and spare parts he might need to fix them. He was ready for anything. Predictably, what was freedom to him seemed enslavement to me, and I throw everything away, as if otherwise one day I'd have to pack it all up and take it through airport security. Child of a later era, I am always trying to travel light, clean up, lose weight, forget. But all these words I'm piling up? They are massless, and besides, the books one takes on that plane are not one's own.

•

Let's not burn that bridge till we cross it.

·

At 10, I'm sure I never had the thought *How much of the past I don't remember!* Even at 20, I assumed it was all down there somewhere, just waiting for the right cue to surface in all its original freshness. Probably my memory was a little sharper then, certainly fewer years were filling it up. But more than that, memory then was spontaneous and passive: it just happened, and the past was whatever I remembered. Now memory is something I actively send back to look for my life, and it returns with unconvincing generalizations—looking out the window, walking to work, Mom.

·

Just on percentages, it's obvious that forgetting is more natural than remembering. And so much of what you remember most vividly serves mainly as a warning against doing again what you're going to want to forget.

·

The self does not exist. But just try to change it.

·

All that reaching for the future: the daydreams, the worry, the waiting, the months I waved away because I just had to finish something. So much of the past has vanished because it was never really the present.

·

I tried. No, to be honest, I tried to try.

·

History repeats itself is roughly analogous to *Language repeats itself.* We've heard it all, but we still don't know what's coming next.

·

My story was that I was past all stories.

•

The books I love best can be read backwards or sideways. Can be read closed or gazing out a window.

•

I try to take it all back, but the tape in reverse is unintelligible.

•

In the long run there was only the short run.

•

Fate? Maybe behind me.

•

Dear Odysseus. These days, you could fly from Troy to Ithaka in an hour. From 40,000 feet, you could see both at once. Just saying.

•

Time hammers with a feather.

•

Less and less of my life lies before me, but always the whole world.

•

Driving, July: *Bridge May Be Icy.*

BRANDEL FRANCE de BRAVO

A Tale of Two Rivers

Washington has always been a tale of two rivers,
what you could call the white river and the black river.

—Jim Dougherty, Sierra Club

1

MANY WHO HAVE WRITTEN ABOUT Washington, D.C.—not as the nation's capital but as a city and permanent home, my home—have used Dickens' *A Tale of Two Cities* as a starting point. Whether side-by-side or nestled one inside the other, there are two Washingtons: a black one, the country's first city with an African-American majority, and a white one, made up mostly of transplants.

I was born here, and I'm white. In the future, many more people will be able to say the same due to gentrification and the resulting black flight. It used to be that when acquaintances asked me where I was from, they assumed "Washington, D.C." was short-hand for one of the Maryland or Virginia suburbs. And the ones who knew something about the geography, knew about Bethesda, Chevy Chase, Falls Church and McLean, would ask: *But where did you really grow up?*

2

LIKE A LOT OF CITIES, Washington, D.C. has two rivers, but they are far from equal in stature. The Potomac River, which separates the city from Virginia and George Washington's riverfront home, Mount Vernon, is the one Robert E. Lee crossed to invade the north. Four hundred and five miles long, it is the "nation's river" and like the Mississippi, it is an "American heritage river."

But it is the less distinguished, long neglected Anacostia River—only 8.7 miles long—that has come to symbolize Washington, D.C.'s racial divide: the population east of it is over 90% African-American. While "east of the river" has become synonymous for some with "high crime" or "under-served," people of varying means reside there. The area includes historic Anacostia where Frederick Douglas lived, the Barry Farm public housing complex (built on the site of the city's first free black settlement), and upper-middle class neighborhoods like Hillcrest, which has been home to at least two mayors.

3

SQUAT BESIDE A RIVER, PEER down, and you can see rocks, silt, green-phantasm-waving, and fish oh-ing, or you can see your reflection. Sometimes when the light and your frame of mind are right, you can see both: you assembling and disassembling with each breeze or insect landing, and beneath that, the inverted firmament. A wet polyphony of present and past, or perhaps present and future.

This is a tale of two rivers, my two rivers. More than that, it is the tale of two Washingtonians who were born and died only a few months apart: one black and one white; one who sang and one who couldn't; one famous; one not; one native-born and the other adopted.

4

THE MAJORITY OF WASHINGTON, D.C., residents are "adopted." In 2010, nearly 63% were born elsewhere, a higher proportion than in any state, except Nevada and Florida.

In "Two Cities in One," Latoya Peterson, owner and editor of Racialicious.com, explains that there is "Washington," and then there is "D.C." "The folks who watch (or are guests on) "Meet the Press'" call it "Washington," but those born to parents from here call it "D.C." Both cities are a state of mind, and inhabitants of either may or may not live within the physical city's limits. Citizens of "Washington" often reside in northern Virginia or Montgomery County, Maryland "for the good public schools," but increasingly they can be found—particularly if childless—in any one of the city's quadrants, including parts of the city that only 2 decades ago were the exclusive domain of D.C.'s citizens, meaning predominantly black neighborhoods.

Today, "D.C." is as likely to exist outside the four quadrants as in them—maybe more so in Maryland's Prince George's County. Even though Prince George's is the wealthiest county in the U.S. with a majority black population, it has also become one of the default destinations for African-Americans who can no longer afford to live in Washington, D.C.

5

IF YOU'VE LIVED ALL YOUR life west of the Anacostia River, when you cross it you may be surprised by the hilltop views afforded of official Washington. "Acropolis" literally means city on a point or "city on the extremity." The area east of the Anacostia River is an acropolis dotted with the ruins of failed solutions, such as St. Elizabeths, the first federally run psychiatric hospital, once known as the Government Hospital for the Insane; the Benning Road Power Plant; and the Kenilworth Landfill with its open incineration. These sites have all been closed or repurposed, but the Anacostia sediments have not forgotten: concentrations of lead, cadmium, zinc, PCBs, and other contaminants continue to be much higher than in the sediments of the Potomac.

The slow-moving Anacostia, frequently described as turbid, is less able to flush out pollutants, which accumulate like grievances. Turbid: thick or opaque as if with roiled sediment (suspended foreign particles); deficient in clarity or purity.

Rated one of the most polluted waterways in the nation, the Anacostia River is a tributary of the Potomac. Even though "the forgotten river" feeds the "nation's river," their fates—like two people the same age living in the same city—are not as intertwined as you might think.

Ruth and Chuck were born June 22nd and August 22nd, 1936. They died at age 75, first Ruth, who was white, and then Chuck, who was black. She died at home, and he in a high-tech medical center. She had lung cancer; he'd been hospitalized for pneumonia, an infection which causes the air sacs and the space between the thin tissues encasing the lungs to fill with fluid.

A river can be a lung.

BUDDHIST MONK AND PEACE ACTIVIST Thich Nhat Hanh writes: "We have to meditate on being the river so that we can experience within ourselves the fears and hopes of the river."

I am looking for stillness in a current of facts. My mantra, if I have one, is the telling.

CHUCK BROWN, "THE GODFATHER OF Go-Go," D.C.'s *sui generis* funk, grew up near the source of the Anacostia, in Prince George's County, but he wasn't born there. Lila Louise Brown gave birth to Chuck in Gaston, North Carolina in 1936. Eight months later, when Chuck's father died of pneumonia, she moved to Charlotte with her baby to find a job. She worked as a live-in maid until she met Chuck's stepfather, and the family moved to Richmond, Virginia. There Chuck's stepfather worked at saw mills, in construction, and at the Lucky Strike cigarette factory.

They lived in shacks on several different Virginia farms. "I used to love to watch the trains go by. I would stand in the field waving and a man on the red caboose would throw me a bag of food every day—potatoes, chicken, biscuits." Chuck learned to sing by going to church with his mother, who not only sang but played harmonica, accordion, and a little piano. He started singing gospel with her when he was only three years old—sometimes for money, sometimes for food.

Oh, that little boy going to be someone someday.

In 1944, Chuck's family headed even further north, leaving the south for good like millions of other African-Americans in what came to be known as the 2nd Great Migration. The family settled in Fairmount Heights, Maryland, just over the D.C. line, 8 miles from the Potomac River.

8

WHAT YOU MIGHT SEE ON the Potomac River: sailboats, rowboats, canoes, sculls, sweeps, kayaks, paddleboards, and power boats with blondes diving from them, cases of beer on board. What you might see in the Anacostia River: folding chairs, barbeque grills, tires, Styrofoam cups, plastic bags, and human feces. Notice the prepositions: "on" and "in."

Ruth Murray was born in Northwest D.C., eight miles from the Anacostia River, and lived there nearly her whole life. Her parents had moved to the capital in the 1920s because her father, a flight instructor and aviation pioneer, had been hired by Boeing, and like every defense contractor, Boeing needed a man in Washington.

Ruth and Chuck were five years-old when Pearl Harbor was bombed. According to Brown, "Mama made me get up under the bed. It was thousands of miles away and I looked out to the window, looking for the bombs." A few months later, Ruth's Japanese housekeeper Gladys was sent to a "War Relocation Camp." Ruth wept for days, and throughout her life she decried the injustice of the internment. She never spoke in as impassioned a way about the civil rights of colored people. If Gladys' abrupt removal was a hole in Ruth's skirt, segregation was the lining. No one saw it unless it came undone.

Even though her father had lost "everything" in the stock market crash, Ruth grew up with nursemaids, cooks, oriental carpets, crystal, and a grand piano. She began weekly lessons when she was seven years-old and was instructed to play for company. Chuck started teaching himself to play at seven, the same age he smoked his first cigarette. By thirteen, Ruth and Chuck had both quit playing.

At age eight, only a river between them, they listened to the Lone Ranger and ate dinners purchased with ration stamps in rooms of invisible light. Every Sunday they went to church: Ruth to St. Anne's with her father, and Chuck and his mother to Mt. Zion Holiness Church. Ruth belonged to a club called the Secret Three: only she and her best friend, Boots, belonged—that was the secret. Chuck's mother bought him a bugle at the Salvation Army, which he played each morning before breakfast to everyone on Jay Street's dismay. Ruth became a Brownie; Chuck started shining shoes. He stationed himself in front of the Howard Theater, the Greyhound Bus Station, the Navy Yard, and in Foggy Bottom where he knelt at the feet of Louie Armstrong, Hank Williams, and Les Paul.

9

A RIVER CAN BECOME AN estuary, emptying into and receiving the sea. Some salt, maybe even a shark, finds its way to the capital. A river appears to flow one way when, in fact, it may be moving in two directions at once.

Eleven years before Ruth and Chuck were born, 25,000 Ku Klux Klan members paraded down Pennsylvania Avenue, past the White House. Three years later, the Klan marched in Washington, D.C. for the last time. There were only a few thousand of them in 1928, but for the first time they marched with their faces uncovered.

These are some of the places where Chuck Brown and Ruth Murray could have met as children:

—at the National Zoo

—in Rock Creek Park

—at Griffith Stadium

—at the National Museum of Natural History

These are some of the places where they could not have met:

—at school

—on a playground

—at the movies

—at the Glen Echo Amusement Park

—rolling Easter eggs on the White House lawn

—over ice cream sundaes at Hecht's Department Store

—watching *Oklahoma* at the National Theater in 1948, just before it closed for three years rather than integrate.

These are a few of the things that happened in 1954 when Ruth and Chuck were eighteen: she rode on the roof of a limousine around the tidal basin wearing a tiara and sash that said "Cherry Blossom Princess, Wyoming"; he, having lived on the streets since thirteen, robbed his first jewelry store in Washington, D.C.; and just as she was graduating from private high school, the Supreme Court ruled that "separate educational facilities are inherently unequal."

Anyone who is around Ruth for more than five minutes becomes acutely aware of her artistic ability. Her incredibly tiny hands are never idle when there is doodling to be done. Another five minutes will reveal Ruth's passion for singing, off tune that is.

Outside of school, the incredibly tiny hands were never without a cigarette.

Dear Ruth,

I'm sure you'll look cute in Bermuda shorts on the Vassar campus. I know I'll be hearing about you and your escapades from half the boys at Harvard. I'm sure you'll know more kids at Harvard than I will. Your cartwheels and modern dance on your porch were wonderful—such form. Next you'll be adopting a Russian accent and trying out for the Ballet Russe.

Love Kent

Ruth,

You and I are no longer on speaking terms since you refused to illustrate my English book! I wonder how long you'll be able to stand it at a girls' school.

Dave

10

The day that Ruth took her final art history exam sophomore year of college, Chuck traded five cartons of cigarettes for a guitar. Six months later, Chuck had learned to play guitar and was performing in front of an audience. After graduating from Vassar, Ruth returned to D.C. to become an artist, although she wasn't exactly sure what that entailed. She married a man from North Carolina named Bill who left her before their baby was born. One of Ruth's few finished paintings is of her young daughter in shades of turmeric.

First, Chuck played with the Earls of Rhythm, then Los Latinos, then the Soul Searchers, until it was Chuck Brown and the Soul Searchers. And then, finally, it was just Chuck Brown.

Ruth dreamed of living in another country, even better, another century. Chuck dreamed of creating a sound for his town, a percussion-driven, call-and-response form of dance music that drew on Afro-Cuban polyrhythms, one song bleeding into another. "I just thought of it because, you know, you got night clubs, go-go clubs, go-go girls dancing in the club but there was no go-go music so I decided to call it go-go music simply because it didn't stop, it just keep going and going and going . . ." Regardless of who he was playing with, Chuck was the guitarist and lead "talker," exhorting people to get on that floor or stay on that floor, and giving shout outs.

"You'd call somebody's name out, that make people feel good when you call their name."

If go-go was playing on someone's car radio or people were dancing to it in the park, Ruth couldn't have told you anything about what she was hearing, except to say it was "loud." She paid no attention to popular music, and if she hummed "Greensleeves" or "Dixie Land," you wouldn't recognize it because she couldn't carry a tune. When everyone in high school was asked their favorite song, she replied: "When I'm not near the boy I love, I love the boy I'm near."

Some of Chuck's hits: "We the People"; "Blow Your Whistle"; "Bustin Loose"; "Day-O"; "Run Joe"; "It don't mean a thing if it ain't got that go-go swing"; "I want some money"; "Wind me Up."

Some of Ruth's men: Judson; Bill; Alec; John.

Chuck Brown's sound caught on with D.C. area bands and became popular. Unlike hip hop or rap, which began in the south Bronx and then coursed through the country and around the world, go-go never really left the "DMV"—the District, Maryland, and Virginia. It made it into the national spotlight only a few times over the years: Spike Lee featured Experience Unlimited's song, "Da Butt" in his 1988 movie, *School Daze*, and in 2010, Chuck Brown's "Bustin' Loose" was used in a TV commercial for Chips Ahoy cookies. In spite of these flings with fame, go-go remains resolutely local: not stagnant but opaque to those not from D.C.

Below is a list of jobs held by Chuck and Ruth. Categorize the status of each by writing a "P" for Potomac or an "A" for Anacostia next to it:

Truck driver   ____

Cashier   ____

Sparring partner   ____

Cocktail waitress   ____

Brick layer   ____

Receptionist   ____

Flight attendant   ____

Newspaper seller   ____

Ice deliverer   ____

Administrative assistant   ____

Watermelon wagon vendor   ____

Coffee house owner   ____

These are the awards and distinctions Chuck earned:

2005: Lifetime Heritage Fellowship Award from the National Endowment for the Arts (NEA).

2009: A section of 7th Street, N.W. between T Street and Florida Avenue is named "Chuck Brown Way."

2011: He is nominated for a Grammy for Best R&B performance by a Duo or Group With Vocals for his collaboration with Jill Scott and Marcus Miller on the song "We Got This."

2012: Ten thousand people line up to view Chuck's body, and flags are flown at half mast throughout the city in honor of the Godfather of Go-Go.

At Chuck's funeral, D.C Council Chair Kwame Brown says, "For all of the people who just moved to Washington, D.C., and have a problem with go-go music, get over it." "Get over it" is what former mayor Marion Barry told white voters when he was elected to political office again after serving time for smoking crack cocaine.

In 2001, Ruth received an award for Distinguished Service to Georgetown, the white neighborhood where she lived, adjacent to the Potomac River. Chair of an historic preservation committee, she was recognized for stopping change, for *not* allowing things to go-go.

11

Ruth and Chuck had something in common: they both had a gap between their two front teeth. In dentistry, this is called diastema, Latin for interval, which can be:

> the difference between two pitches
> a pause or break
> an intervening time or space

There was an interval—a year—when Ruth and Chuck's lives could have intersected, when two rivers might have met.

In 1959, Ruth and her husband Bill Walker opened Washington, D.C.'s first poetry and jazz coffee house—first at 912 New Hampshire Avenue and then at 945 K Street. Coffee 'n Confusion was a sensation, and its happenings and recurring legal battles were frequently reported on in *The Washington Post* and other local newspapers.

> *Event No. 1 was an early evening announcement that beat Washington poets would pit their lines against some beat New York poets. Washington won, man! The New Yorkers failed to show. Admission to the poetry reading contest was $1 a head and there was standing room only for the press. The bearded Walker called the formalities to order against the background music of a set of jungle drums, and within minutes even they were silent.*

Eventually, the out-of-town poets, including Leroi Jones—soon to be Amiri Baraka—and Allen Ginsberg, showed up. Ruth didn't like any of the poetry recited, muttered, screamed, declaimed, incanted at Coffee 'n Confusion, not even her husband's: *Mrs. Walker prefers John Donne to the "beat" poets and she's certain Proust had more on the ball than Kerouac.*

She went along with the coffeehouse, playing hostess in a black leotard, auburn hair down her back, because people like her, she reasoned, needed a place to gather and discuss art and literature the way she and her friends had done at college, in their pajamas. And she went along with it because Bill wanted it.

Coffee 'n Confusion wasn't at all as Ruth had imagined. The poets were "inebriated or high on something, and there was a lot of posturing and fighting," and unlike at Vassar, the women were minor characters, as in the book of the same title by Kerouac's ex, Joyce Johnson. When she wasn't busy playing hostess, she was bailing Bill out of jail or appearing by his side in court.

But the coffeehouse was one of the few venues in 1950s Washington where whites—at least the kind who appreciated "jungle drums"—and blacks mingled. Mississippi John Hurt, Dizzie Gillespie, Miles Davis, and Fats Domino performed at Coffee 'n Confusion or stopped in to hear one another play. Anyone as talented as Chuck Brown who heard about this scene would have wanted to check it out, maybe even get a gig there. After all, by 1959, Chuck had not only mastered the guitar but was entertaining large and very appreciative crowds.

Unfortunately, the crowds consisted of incarcerated men.

12

IN 1959, CHUCK WAS HALFWAY through his eight-year prison term. Back when Ruth was still a cheerleader in high school, Chuck had graduated from shooting craps and hustling pool to robbery, sometimes armed. One night in 1954, Ruth was loading trunks filled with her clothes for college into the car, and Chuck shot a man in self-defense. The wounded man later died, and Chuck's aggravated assault sentence was commuted to murder. He was sentenced to a facility in Virginia operated by the D.C. Department of Corrections: the Lorton Reformatory.

In Lorton, Chuck paid a fellow prisoner, a man named Bunny, five cartons of cigarettes for a guitar Bunny had made in shop. Chuck plucked and strummed on his bunk until he knew the six strings better than his six-digit ID number, and soon he was famous inside Lorton, where he returned regularly after his release to play for the inmates.

When Chuck walked out a free man in 1962: "I took that guitar with me and I used to play in peoples' backyards, cooker house and things like that and people would invite me to their house . . . I wasn't allowed to play in any places that sold alcoholic beverages."

In 1962, Ruth was free, too: two years after Bill Walker had fled D.C., having signed over Coffee 'n Confusion to a man with mafia connections, and two years after their daughter was born, Ruth's divorce was finalized. And just as Chuck was getting out of Lorton, Bill Walker was entering Madrid's Carabanchel prison, along with his pregnant girlfriend.

By the time Chuck died, he had recorded more than 20 albums and sold 1.5 million copies since his first hit record in 1971, "We the People."

"There was a time when the only people who wanted to take my picture was the police. Now, the police want to take pictures with me . . . "

How you see the river depends on which side you live on. A river can be a border, telling us where we begin or end. The river we call the "Rio Grande," the Mexicans call the "Rio Bravo." One country calls the river big, and the other calls it tough, wild, brave.

13

IN SOME CULTURES A SPACE between the two front teeth means you will be wealthy, lucky, or if you are a woman, lustful. *I know I'll be hearing about you and your escapades from half the boys at Harvard.*

Ruth and Chuck died—if not wealthy—with means. Were they lucky, too?

Ruth was inside the about to-be-opened Coffee 'n Confusion, painting a mural, when a bullet punctured the plate-glass window, missing her head by inches.

Police said the shots came from the gun of Louis Engle, 37, of the 1000 block of K street N.W. who is licensed as a medium at that address . . . "I just don't like beatniks," police quoted Mr. Engle.

If Ruth was fortunate that the fortune-teller had poor aim, perhaps it was fun-nel-shaped luck that lifted Chuck from the streets, landing him behind bars. "But when I went to Lorton, that's where I found myself." He obtained a high school diploma, a guitar, and he got his gift for music back. *Oh, that little boy going to be someone someday.* Long before his death, he'd joined the ranks of Duke Ellington, Billy Eck-stine, Roberta Flack, Marvin Gaye, and all the other Washingtonians who've made musical history.

When Chuck Brown was hospitalized with pneumonia, the entire city was on alert, in-cluding the mayor, the newspapers and radio stations. He died surrounded by friends, his wife, Jocelyn, and four of his children.

Ruth died in a narrow, one-bedroom apartment, her last man by her side. Other than the hospice nurse and her daughter, she almost never had visitors. After *The Girl with the Dragon Tattoo*, *The Girl Who Played with Fire*, *The Girl Who Kicked the Hornet's Nest*, when she could no longer read, she wrote sequels in her head until the morphine made even that impossible. This is how she chose to go: the water that is a human body evaporating into air, her four-poster a dry river bed.

Who is the national river? Who is the forgotten river? To this day there are arguments over which is the world's longest river. Calculating this is difficult because it depends on pinpointing a beginning and end.

14

WHILE MIX TAPES OF GO-GO continue to be a local industry, it is music meant to be heard live. It is about "being there" and more specifically about being *here*: in D.C. and the surrounding areas of Maryland and Virginia. The crews, the streets, the neighbor-hoods, the names being called out don't mean anything to people not from "around the way." Because it is music by and mainly for black people, its popularity confined to a small section of the mid-Atlantic, go-go is more "Anacostia" than "Potomac." And just as the Anacostia has been a repository for the city's darkness—that which is cast off, toxic—go-go bore the blame for much of the violence here in the late 80s and early 90s. Even today, communities are wary of it: many African-American residents of the Langdon neighborhood where a park has been named after Chuck Brown have opposed the proposed amphitheater, fearing that performances there would be too disruptive or bring trouble.

But the sound Chuck Brown created for his town will live on, as the name go-go implies, evolving into "bounce beat" and whatever comes after that, and after that. "Most public high schools in the eastern part of D.C. and in neighboring Prince George's County have go-go bands, just as most high schools in New Orleans have brass bands," writes Natalie Hopkinson in her book, *Go-Go Live*.

From corrections to curriculum, from prison to tradition: Chuck Brown, American heritage river?

Like go-go, Coffee 'n Confusion was a local phenomenon. What fame it had outside of Washington, D.C. was eclipsed by the bookstores, cafes, night clubs and churches of New York and San Francisco. When writing about the notorious but brief-lived Coffee 'n Confusion, reporters often commented on Ruth's striking appearance and her privilege: *The Vassar College graduate startled the usual crowd of policemen, defendants and hangers-on by strolling in wearing a green sweater ensemble, a plaid skirt to match—and no shoes.*

But in spite of her advantages, Ruth's life was sometimes difficult and mostly unremarkable. She was a single mother when that bordered on scandalous for someone white and upper-middle-class, and when resources for working mothers were scarcer even than they are today. Half of every paycheck went to the black women—Howard University students, tired grandmothers—who showed up each morning to care for her daughter.

Ruth's was a tributary life: hours streaming into jobs that demanded little creativity, days meandering as they fed a next life. She eventually found her artistic calling, a way to busy her fingers once they no longer held a cigarette. Five years into jewelry making, she was diagnosed with lung cancer.

The Anacostia won't be fishable or swimmable until 2032, but the Anacostia Waterfront is now, says the D.C. government, "the fastest growing area of employment, entertainment, and residential growth."

15

THEIR NAMES METRICALLY SIMILAR, EACH a spondee in two very different poems, Ruth France and Chuck Brown lived nearly all of their 75 years in the same city without ever meeting, two rivers without confluence. Two Washingtonians: one native-born, the other not; one black and one white; one who sang and one who couldn't; one famous, the other not.

A man I never met whose music I loved, and my mother. This is a tale of the two rivers that ran through Chuck and Ruth, that run, like hope and fear, through me.

When I left Washington, D.C. for college at seventeen, I never thought I'd return. I equated staying with stagnation. It was what my mother had done. After twenty-two years away, I came back. Now, with no family left here, and my daughter about to leave for college, I ask myself: should I stay? To allow yourself to be *of* a place, to own it and let it own you, has its recompense: knowledge accumulates, relationships deepen, and changes—to your city, to you, your body and mind—are more easily observed. But to leave and start over in a new place is to be reborn: the challenge, and even stress of it, rejuvenating. While moving again and again prevents you from ever getting truly comfortable, it also lets you live a lie.

When Chuck Brown and Ruth France smiled, you noticed the gap. The space between their two front teeth was strangely alluring. You noticed the way an absence can separate and draw you in. Stare hard enough and you just might find stillness.

JILL KHOURY

Cranial Nerve II
the optic nerve

If the axon thicket
        does not flourish
the child will be IRREVERSIBLY BLIND.

      : and the kingdom weeps :

Say *lack of thread*

      : make it a romance :

Say *dead just dead*

      : moonless sky :

Say *hypoplasia*

      : In the coppice waits a deer   He rubs his antlers on a tree :

Say *usually correlated with other central nervous system defects*

      : Grew up near a river alongside the thalamus :

      : we are waiting for our :

Girl in a white robe with feathers
Girl with a knapsack stepping off a cliff
Girl with a picnic basket containing cake and wine
Girl cyborg in black stilettos
Girl with the face of a honey-colored dog
Girl on the cover of a charity website looks like me

      I was one of the lucky ones

I wasn't one of the lucky ones

: and the huntsman took scissors and cut open your mother's belly :

nonetheless
the fact is that
even so
nonwithstanding
equanimitably
in spite of
unassumedly
because why wouldn't I

: girl wakes up in a spare circle of saplings :

Ask *can she see*

JEFFREY MORGAN

Immunity

A little bit of sky gets sucked up into the syringe
with the dead flu.

It all depends
on your definition of where the sky begins. I've passed out

more than once while blood was being drawn,
but I don't mind

getting shots, or even tattoos. It makes sense to me
that there's a phobic difference
between addition and subtraction.

Many of our best buildings are shaped like needles,
and we are like platelets
running around trying to stop something, but what?

Sometimes nurses must see in the thin arms of winter trees
patients they have known.

We take the work home.
We tell our lovers
and our lovers tell us, our works marry
in the contagion of listening.

The nurse taps the syringe to loose the sky.

The best days are the days you call in sick
even though you are fine.

Translation

What I love about St. Sebastian is not the colander the arrows made
of his body, or how he is always shown riddled and tied
to a column, which I should be able to identify
as Doric, Ionic, or Corinthian—
possibly the most pedantic and predictable question
on any art history exam. No. What I love about St. Sebastian
is the painting of him by Mantegna
where he seems to be listening to the sky
the way you or I might listen
to a boss who has no idea what we really do around here.
There is the arrow beneath the right calf
and the arrow through the torso.
Maybe Saints are just like regular people, only better
at remembering things. If you have a lot of things
to memorize, imagine a building you know well.
You know every room and all the furniture.
Place what you want to remember, for example,
in the fifth drawer of your childhood dresser
below where you have left a picture of each type of column
and all the letters in the word *chiaroscuro*.
Store the arrow there until you need it.
Then, you can pull it all the way back to your ear
whenever you want, your body like the dissipating vibrations of a string.
It is especially the last note that becomes its listener.

JEHANNE DUBROW

SOS

Distress is signaled by a run of threes:
three dits three dahs three dits, and then it all
begins again. The meaning of this call
for help can be discerned in its reprise.
No matter where the listener starts, the pleas
for help—*please help me please*—repeat their small
alert. The ship is threatened by a squall.
The ship is lost, has suffered casualties.
If we are ships we too have signaled land
or called each other in the dark. We've scanned
the sky for help. We've said *emergency,*
a sequence made of silences and tones.
And when it ends, we've said *seelonce feenee.*
The sea says nothing back. The anchor groans.

STEFANIE WORTMAN

The Gossip Machine

Like an old fashioned
        telephone with a cone you disclose
your desire for news
        to and a wired horn which conveys
the same to your ear.
        It has a dial you can turn for more
erotic detail.
        A man can whisper the suspicions
he holds about his
        wife and the indifferent instrument
will return to him
        her image in another bedroom,
pink, postcoitally
        serene. A woman can ask about her
lover, looking for
        the one who taught him to love a slap
in the face. The thing
        will proffer a name but no reason.
The voice that speaks is
        not male or female, just a pressure
device appended
        to facscimile lips and mobile
tongue. If some refrain
        from touching the machine for ethics
or kindness, if some
        turn in disgust, unwilling to suffer
these secrets, the rest,
        like me, want to exhaust everything
it has to offer.

JOHN KOETHE

Idiot Wind

Another idiot denounces American poets:
Give us more of the "we" we need, he demands,
And I agree, but so what? I do it constantly,
And I'm not alone. And yet we're so abstract,
So dispersed, so virtual I don't know who "we" are—
Not other poets certainly, or the people in the theaters
I frequent on weekends, watching movies of exploding trucks.
My mother weaned me on Emerson, though I didn't know it,
And Emerson (no idiot) railed against American poets too:
"Men of talents who sing, and not the children of music.
The argument is secondary, the finish of the verses primary."
I omitted an "is" in that quotation for the sake of finish,
And yet I think a poem *should* be the "metre-making argument"
Emerson called for, though the argument always peters out.
We try and try, and try and try again to get it right
Along the road to hell, but it never works: something
Off to one side derails it, or it loses focus, or the better angels
Of our nature wake, and then go back to sleep. Poems
Should be true, true to what we think—"to thine own self
Be true"—but then, what do we think? We reason in clichés—
Otherwise, we'd never move. Why should we deny
This truth about ourselves? Can't we see what we are?

ROBERT ARCHAMBEAU

Hating the Other Kind of Poetry

1. THIS IS NOT A HOW-TO GUIDE

It isn't quite a how-not-to guide either, but I suppose that's closer.

2. "WHAT YOU *SHOULD* BE DOING," OR: THE LIMITS OF DISINTEREST

A few years ago, when the Conceptualist poet Kenneth Goldsmith was making big waves in the little demitasse cup of the American poetry world, I wrote an essay that tried to explain what his work had to offer and what it didn't. The email I received in response was gratifying in quantity, if bewildering in content. I'd tried merely to describe Goldsmith's work, but I found I was condemned for having praised him, praised for having condemned him, praised for having praised him, and condemned for having condemned him—all in roughly equal measure. The uniform distribution of responses on the chart of praise and blame gave me some reassurance that my attempt at mere description hadn't unintentionally become a clear act of advocacy or disapproval, but it also confirmed my suspicion that people were not particularly inclined to view as innocent an essay that did its best to remain neutral: an agenda, the thinking went, must lurk just below the surface. I am not so naïve as to believe that truly disinterested inquiry is possible, but the notion that we may approach disinterest asymptotically—like a curving line that comes ever closer to another line without ever touching it—was clearly alien to a literary audience that had been through several decades of the hermeneutics of suspicion. Only M, a critic from whom I had learned a great deal over the years, and who had always been kind to me, saw the essay for what it was, or tried to be—and she didn't like it. "What you *should* be doing," she told me, "is making a strong case for the poetry you believe in, and against the poetry you don't." She'd been doing exactly that for decades, and I knew people who revered her for it. I also knew people people who all but spat when they said her name.

3. "THAT NEVER WORKS," OR: PLURALISM AND FAILURE

It wasn't the first time I'd been told something like that. Back in the final decade of the last century, when I was starting up a little magazine devoted to poetry, I received much helpful advice from K, a poet and critic who, like M, had long championed the more experimental wing of poetry. I was young and dewy-eyed, and had the usual delusions about what a little magazine might accomplish. "What I really want to do," I said, over coffee in some dingy university café, "is make a space for different kinds of poets to come together and talk to one another." "Yeah," said K, my senior by a decade and a grizzled veteran of the long march of experimental poetry from the wilderness into the academy, "that never works."

Years later, long after the fate of my magazine had proved K right, I was in touch with him again, this time after the early death of another poet, a tremendously charming American who'd moved to London and written formal verse in traditional rhyme and meter. He and K had been friends in their grad school days—"dope smoking buddies, mostly," as K put it—but had, despite a few joyous reunions when all arguments were put aside, fallen out over poetry. They hadn't seen each other in years, and the news of the poet's death hit K hard. "I always thought there'd come a time when all these poetry wars would be behind us, and we'd be friends again" he told me. I didn't know what to say.

4. "I find your paper irritating," or: looking at the back of your own head

I don't remember what I said, and that's not what's important anyway: what's important is the aftermath. I was standing rather smugly before an audience at an academic conference where I'd just delivered a paper on a poet of some repute, fielding questions along with the other panelists, when I saw the formidable white mane of C rise above the crowd. A scholar whose elegant suits and forceful manner gave him an aura closer to that of a Mafiosi than one would have thought possible for a professor of literature, C did not look happy, and he was looking at me. "I find your paper irritating," he said. "Don't misunderstand: I liked the other papers more, but didn't find them interesting enough to be irritating. Come to think of it, I didn't find your paper interesting either—it's the nature of my irritation with it that's interesting."

In the well-crafted spoken paragraphs that followed, C took my paper apart, but he did much more than that: he also disassembled his own reaction to my paper, pulled out the assumptions behind that reaction, held them up to the sunlight and saw what was beautiful and meaningful in those assumptions, and what was narrow and even cruel. It was magnificent. With the possible exception of the time an esteemed English editor took a cricket bat to some of my prose and beat it into a wet pulp from which he then formed a proper essay, C's takedown of my paper remains my favorite literary chastening. It also showed me something one could do with a text that wasn't advocacy (it was about as far from advocacy of what I'd said as one could get) and wasn't simply condemnation either. Nor was it disinterested or neutral explanation, of the sort I'd tried to supply in my essay on Goldsmith, and it certainly wasn't any sort of pluralistic live-and-let-live move, either. In the encounter with an irritating text, C had taken a step back and seen not only the irksome text in front of him, but seen himself looking at it. It was as if he stood behind himself, looking at the back of his own head. *Ekstasis*, the ancient Greeks called it—standing outside oneself. It was C's interpretive ecstasy, and we watched in wonder.

5. "That fucking Merwin," or: the back of Creeley's head

I know a lot of people who loved Robert Creeley, who saw the old sage of Black Mountain and Buffalo as a generous mentor and friend, and he certainly was that. He may turn out to have meant more to more younger poets than any other figure of his generation. But if you read his letters, you see that he had as large a capacity for hatred as he had for paternal or avuncular love. He despises Theodore Roethke and Louis Simpson, hurls abuse at Helen Vendler, spews bile in the direction of Louise Glück and Charles Wright, dismisses Kenneth Koch as a lightweight, and talks about cutting Frank O'Hara (the editors of the letters work hard, in a footnote, to explain this away as metaphorical, and may be right). "Fuck him," he says of Kenneth Patchen, and he tells us how "that fucking Merwin" is a "a symbol of rot." He clearly sees battle lines drawn between a kind of poetry he admires and the kinds he does not, and he takes exception when the people who should be on his side appear to cross the line and embrace the enemy. "I will never forget this," he writes to Kenneth Rexroth, when the older poet treasonously supported Roethke; and when William Carlos Williams spoke approvingly of W. H. Auden, Creeley demanded to know whether someone had held a gun to Williams' back. Academics have a special place in Creeley's inferno—even after so many of them had come to accept his views about who the important poets were. In 1985, he tells us that academics wouldn't deign to write about Williams or Olson—and does so with such vehemence that I wouldn't want to have been the one to tell him of the half dozen prominent academic articles on Olson that year alone, or the three dozen on Williams, or of the professor who'd just edited the sixth volume of Creeley's correspondence with Olson. Resentment outlives its occasion, and those who harbor it don't want to be reminded of the fact.

When I've mentioned this vituperative side of Creeley to his old friends and allies, they've been quick to point out that Creeley and the poets he supported were for a long time—and in some quarters are even now—the subject of a disdain every bit as strong as that which we find in Creeley's letters. They're not wrong, these friends of Creeley. You won't find as much invective about Creeley and his peers in the letters of those about whom he snarled, except perhaps in recent years, but that's simply because silence is the snarling of the powerful.

What, I wonder, would Creeley have seen if he'd looked, not at those he despised, but at himself looking at them? What if, like C, he had seen himself from outside himself? I suppose he'd have seen a man in something like the condition Pierre Bourdieu describes when he discusses what happens to an art when it is no longer playing for stakes beyond art itself in any meaningful way—when there are few significant financial, political, or ecclesiastical rewards at stake, when it operates at the margins of money and power. Under these conditions, it is the practitioners of the art itself who hand out the rewards, and while those rewards may be in some minimal sense matters of money or power or hierarchical position, they are primarily matters of recognition. No one's been made a lord for poetry since Tennyson, and no one hoping for riches nowadays would present a poem to a head of state, as Edmund Spenser did—successfully—to Elizabeth I. Bourdieu tells us that when the practitioners of an art become the primary decision makers about who gets the (largely symbolic) rewards, we see a phenomenon called "the social aging of art." This is a process in which one group—generally marginal, young, or both—seeks to discredit those who practice the art differently. One doesn't compete for money in a commercial market, but for prestige in a symbolic market, and the way to do that isn't to woo customers, but to discredit the other guys. It's no accident that the proliferation of manifestos and aesthetic dogmas came about at the moment when complex developments in mass education, publishing, and communications rendered poetry unviable as a market commodity. Freed from external demands—another way of saying "left to fend for themselves"—the poets proliferated styles and frequently looked with disdain at those whose work took a different path than their own. "That fucking Merwin," one might utter of another.

6. Conquistadors and Anthropologists

The Polish philosopher Leszek Kołakowski once wrote with apparent sympathy of a group of people who believed fervently in their own ideals and disdained those of others, saying:

> A few years ago I visited the pre-Columbian monuments in Mexico and was lucky enough, while there, to find myself in the company of a well known Mexican writer, thoroughly versed in the history of the Indian peoples of the region. Often in the course of explaining to me the significance of many things I would not have understood without him, he stressed the barbarity of the Spanish soldiers who had ground the Aztec statues into dust and melted down the exquisite gold figurines to strike with the image of the Emperor.

I said to him, "you think these people were barbarians; but were they not, perhaps, true Europeans, indeed the last true Europeans? They took their Christian and Latin civilization seriously; and it is because they took it seriously that they saw no reason to safeguard pagan idols; or to bring the curiosity and aesthetic detachment of archeologists into their consideration of things imbued with a different, and therefore hostile religious significance. If we are outraged at their behavior it is because we are indifferent, both to their civilization, and to our own."

Kołakowski was, however, playing devil's advocate—since, for him, the better angels of European civilization were not the conquistadors, but the anthropologists. "The anthropologist," Kołakowski writes,

must suspend his own norms, his judgments, his mental, moral, and aesthetic habits in order to penetrate as far as possible into the viewpoint of another and assimilate his way of perceiving the world. And even though no one, perhaps, would claim to have achieved total success in this effort, even though total success would presuppose an epistemological impossibility—to enter entirely into the mind of the object of inquiry while maintaining the distance and objectivity of the scientist—the effort is not in vain. We cannot completely achieve the position of an observer seeing himself from the outside, but we may do so partially.

Like the scholar C after he heard my irritating paper at the conference years ago, when confronted with that which is alien to our sensibilities we may make the attempt to stand outside ourselves, and in doing so see something other than an object of disdain. Indeed, we may get a kind of doubled or even tripled vision: we'll know the thing we're looking at—a poem, say—on something like its own terms, as well as on ours. Moreover, we might discover something about our own assumptions—our assumptions and, one hopes, ourselves.

7. The potter's wheel and the back of my own head

When I wrote "one hopes" in the previous sentence, I suppose what I really meant was "I hope." But why hope for this kind of approach to poetry, as opposed to the naked partisanship of M or of K? Perhaps the explanation is generational: both M and K are older than I am, and I'm deeper into middle age than I care to admit. The names I recognized among those who wrote to praise or blame me for my article on Goldsmith belonged to an older set, too.

Perhaps as the memory of the exclusion of one sort of poet from the privileged world of academe becomes less a living thing, and more a matter of history, the rhetoric of partisanship will fade. Creeley could still feel marginal even after he was a Chancellor of the Academy of American Poets and a leading figure in the best-funded poetry program in the country, but that was because his formative experiences were those of a truly marginalized outcast. Nowadays, when I read screeds against the Poetry Foundation by full professors at top MFA programs, I suspect what I'm seeing are the last embers of the old fires of outsider resentment. The revolution of the young against the old and the new against the outmoded described by Pierre Bourdieu—the revolution that launched a thousand manifestoes and set anthologists at one another's throats—was the product of a climate of resource scarcity. When there were virtually no external rewards for poets, or when the few rewards (steady teaching jobs, say) were monopolized by a single group (let's call them the poets associated with the New Criticism), partisanship could rage, resentments flare, and those who wrote poetry different from one's own could very easily be cursed as lightweights and symbols of rot. But when academe has long since made room for poets as diverse as Rae Armantrout, Billy Collins, Claudia Rankine, and Kenneth Goldsmith, it's harder to rage convincingly against a monolithic establishment. At least it is for the moment: perhaps the crumbling of the academic humanities will give us a renewed outbreak of heartfelt resentment.

Maybe, though, it's not generational: maybe it's just me. When I ask myself why I resist M's injunction to fight for the kind of poetry I find appealing, and against those kinds to which I am not immediately drawn, the first thing I think of is not my generation, or those coming after me. The first thing I think of is my father, bent over his potter's wheel. Dad is a ceramic artist, and I spent my pre-teen years as an art-school brat of the 1970s—or, to be more precise, as a *provincial* art-school brat of the 1970s, dad being a professor at the deeply rusticated University of Manitoba. What this means is simple: I saw a lot of abstract painters, earthwork sculptors, conceptual artists, installation artists, photorealists and post-minimalists jockeying around for fame and position, hoping like hell to get themselves off the Canadian prairies and back to the American east coast or at the very least to L.A., the kind of cultural centers from whence they'd come. My father had made the opposite move, leaving the faculty of the prestigious Rhode Island School of Design for the boondocks, in part because, like all ceramic artists (and unlike those post-minimalists and conceptualists), he harbored no illusions about becoming any kind of art star. Outside of Japan and a few other Asian cultures, there's simply no prestige to pottery, and no amount of raging or resentment will change that. Creeley could go from the outside in, railing at his enemies all the way, but there's a notable lack of revolutionary rhetoric among ceramicists, who experience the climate of non-recognition as a permanent condition, not as an injustice to be combatted. Most of our attitudes are absorbed from our environment without much conscious reflection on our part, and I imagine my distaste for battles about aesthetic recognition and campaigns against forms of art different from one's own comes less from all those grad school hours reading Bourdieu and Adorno than from seeing my dad roll his eyes at the rhetoric and ambitious yearnings of his colleagues.

Whether the resistance to partisan polemic is a matter of generational and institutional change, or simply a matter of my own peculiar formation, I don't know. I do know that my own resistance to polemic is strong enough that I don't even want this essay to be an advocacy of one approach to poetry over another, although at some level I suppose it inevitably is. What I want this essay to be is less a program than an examination—an attempt to look directly (and impossibly) at the back of my own head.

MARY KURYLA

The Contract

November 1, 1932

To Mr. Wade
Huron Outing and Sporting Club
Onaway, Michigan

I did not do what I was hired to do. We are agreed on that, Mr. Wade. Legally, you don't owe me a red cent. By natural rights, you owe me a million of them, not to mention a new leg for my trouble. So pay attention. I did not come by this conclusion blind, like some who look at a thing until they cannot make of it heads or tails or heads again. My own attorney has told me to write this clear and complete record of events as I witnessed them, sticking just to the facts, and leaving nothing out. I am leaving NOTHING out, Mr. Wade, unlike before when I testified.

Sure enough, we had a contract, Mr. Wade, and it got broken but maybe there was good reason. The only other contract I know is my birth certificate and though some may say that's not a contract, I say why not, it can be broken. Turns out, maybe that birth certificate was broken for good reason, too.

Mr. Wade, you hired me for the job because you said I look where others stop at polite. You said, Look at the man.

How could I not? The head was so askew that under the chin a black scab stuck with a bit of asswiping tissue exposed a morning shave gone wrong. The other side of the man's head gushed blood from a wound sparkling with shards of bottle glass.

Is this man E.Z. Ulrich or not? you said.

Why not ask his wife?

We don't want to distress the lady, your attorney said. See her husband like this. Anyhow, you're just about next of kin.

Okay, I said. But I took my time, Mr. Wade, because we both knew I was doing you a good turn when by natural rights it should have been his wife identifying him.

Wipe that smile off your face, you said. It's indecent to laugh at a dead man.

But Attorney Martin standing there beside you in the clubhouse of the Huron Outing and Sporting Club knew it to be one occasion when laughing did no harm. The harm had already been done when E.Z. Ulrich had come to the clubhouse un-invited and accidentally fallen and struck his head against the sink. Or that's how you told it. Where all the broken glass came from was none of my business. You said that, too.

Get on with it, Simpson, you said, as your fingers flipped the nickels in your pocket.

My gloating over E.Z.'s dead body surprised you, as you probably recall. Truth is, it surprised me, too. E.Z.'s shirt had come unbuttoned at the collar and I squatted beside him to button it up so that he looked more presentable.

That's E.Z. Ulrich, all right, I said.

You looked at me differently after that, Mr. Wade. You took an interest. The moon hardly had time to wax after the Ulrich inquest before you came round offering me a job. Your attorney Martin would draft the contract, and I was to meet him at the clubhouse where I would read it over and sign.

The contract stated the following: "I, Simpson Willis, agree to secure the permanent evacuation of Mrs. Lottie Ulrich from her residence, which shall be known here as 1555 Crooked Lake Lane, by any means at my disposal, for which services Mr. Harry Wade will compensate the amount of one-thousand dollars."

When instead of signing I inquired after your attorney's moustache, how he primped it so narrow, that testy fellow just hollered at me to sign and leave the contract on the table.

I said, You going to sign it first?

Attorney Martin scratched your signature on the line.

What do you want with Lottie's land? I said.

The view, Simp.

He left, saying he'd be back for the contract.

Martin had a point about the clubhouse needing a view. That little kitchen where I sat was as played out as a whore's mattress. Dishes piled in the sink past the clubhouse's only window, grimed with insect shells. Dotting the floor were animal droppings, and vegetable matter curled beneath a fallen and empty whiskey bottle like it might tote the thing away. Darts dug in everywhere except the Union Jack dartboard that hung on the wall beside the great head of a stuffed moose—this in a room hardly big enough to accommodate E.Z. Ulrich's body when it had sprawled across it not a month before. Such squalor must have appealed to your former bachelor days. Pardon me, it's attorney Martin who's married. You are still a bachelor, Mr. Wade. Don't you have the eye of every God-fearing Lutheran widow up and down the state of Michigan?

If you believe that a dwelling squirrels away a few seeds of the wrong done inside it, you'd understand why I grabbed up that contract and left the clubhouse lickety-split. And got right on the job. After all, Ulrich's house was on the way to that shit for shack where I reside with Nanny Furze, the woman who raised me from a child when my own mother, Lottie Ulrich, who was now E.Z.'s widow, gave me up for good.

The sun came and went through the canopy of aspen overhead. I swatted at the black flies along the lane. Pinecones clattered to the ground. As you are no doubt aware, our tallest pines encircle Lottie's clapboard house. I kept clear of the porch, front door too. The floor of pine needles muffled my footsteps. The only sound was of her rowboat scrubbing against the dock by the lily pads blooming in the shallows on the other side of the house. Otherwise, the silence and stillness said Lottie wasn't home. I sidled up to a pair of green shutters on the east side of her two-story. Lacy curtains fluffed at a window left ajar. The bed in Lottie's room stood wide in a wrought iron frame of roses and vines with the robin's egg blue paint worn to white in spots. Unmade, the layers of patchwork quilt and coral woolen blanket and white lace sheet jumbled around a cast-off nightgown of negligee transparency. Above the bed hung a crucifix bout the size of a man's hand. She is a Catholic. A pair of hip boots straddled a chair and a key jammed the lock of a steel green tackle box on the nightstand. The wide mouth of every bass in Black River seems to drop open when Lottie casts her line.

Puddingstones encircled the lamp on the nightstand, the Christmas red of the conglomerate rock warm as the woolen in her bed. Lottie's land is the only to yield up the puddingstone, as you know, Mr. Wade, as well you know. Puddingstone. That's what you were after, wasn't it? Had the rumors of the stone's value lit even your fire? Relocating the clubhouse onto the Ulrich land had nothing to do with its natural beauty. Once you got the rights to the land, you'd probably dig the pudding out, to the last pebble, leaving a great maw that only the turgid waters of Crooked Lake would fill. Attorney Martin had told a fib on your behalf. Though I wished you had seen fit to tell me the truth, arriving at it now perfumed with greater pungency the task of removing Lottie from the home she'd shared with E.Z.

No point loitering further at her window. After all it's not polite to stare. But that photograph stuck in her looking glass of E.Z. Ulrich young and fine in uniform seemed so changed from when I'd last seen it that I stayed to try and work out why. A few years had passed since I'd last ducked the swing of Nanny Furze's corn broom and sneaked over here to where Lottie was making house with the man who made a good woman out of her when he come home from France. Folks say that's where E.Z. learned the damper trade, though in France he was starting fires to smoke out the enemy instead of fighting fires like he did around here.

Breathe in enough smoke, the body goes to sleep. E.Z. had lain on the hook rug a few feet from the very window where I now stood. Lottie's fingers undid the buttons of his shirt, cindery as if he'd followed Saint Nick down the chimney though in fact he'd just damped down that fire in the preserve across the lake, one button undone after another until the white skin shone like chestnut meat under the blackened garment. Lottie kneeling before him with a damp cloth, wiping the black off his face with such tenderness, Mr. Wade, like he was newly born. Receiving all that mothering that by rights belonged to me revived him like an ointment. E.Z.'s eyes opened bright and possessive on her as his hand touched her high cheek, the thumb drawing a black line down her jaw and neck as it found her breast. Lottie looked over her shoulder just then at what must have been the peculiar sound I was making at her window but I managed to light out. I made a pact with myself that night to stop wanting what I cannot have. If I never saw E.Z. Ulrich again I'd be a better man for it.

And that's what I was, a better man—until you called me in to identify him. Did you know when you asked that I had wanted E.Z. Ulrich dead even more than you? Of course you did. A businessman knows what's required to get what he wants. But did you know I'd been waiting on an opportunity to turn Lottie Ulrich out of that house ever since she'd turned me out of hers when I was not much more than a babe pinned up in diapers?

That's when it hit me. The picture of E.Z. had not changed—I had. I'd grow unnatural, and the one to blame was Lottie Ulrich. Red, red, red, that's all I saw as I turned from her window and headed back along the trail, not stopping until I tripped over the tree roots strangling Nanny Furze's cabin. Passing through the door without a nod to the woman winking into her everlasting cauldron of bone marrow soup, I groped for my bed situated in the far corner of the kitchen, dropped to the floor, and crabbed underneath the mattress to where I keep things hidden from Nanny Furze's eye. She's only got the one.

The Good Book, which my mother had tucked in my swaddle blanket the day she handed me off, served as my first reading primer. I held the very same book now in my hands as I leafed through to Revelations, where my birth certificate was hid. "Simpson Willis, born January 1, 1911, to Lottie Willis, mother." Perhaps if I were not so inclined to look where others stop at polite, as you say, Mr. Wade, I might have cried for the years of growing I had done in this shack, which have really been more of a lessening under the eye of Nanny Furze, or I might have cried for the girl of fifteen that Lottie was when she bore me, but I did not. I just stared into the black facts. You, Mr. Wade, wanted Lottie out. I, Mr. Wade, wanted to punish Lottie for not raising me and instead lavishing affection onto E.Z. Ulrich.

Right then I snuck your contract out from beneath my duck canvas coat. With my back to Nanny Furze, I pressed it flat against the pages of the Good Book and signed my name on the dotty line.

And headed back to 1555 Crooked Lake Lane. Only this time I took my time. How would I scare Lottie Ulrich sufficient to give up on her home? Get quiet enough out on the trail and a breeze always comes up. Through the aspen I glimpsed a beaver separating the surface of the lake like a furred zipper and above the tree line something circled the great palm of the lake, its low-slung feathers shuttering the lowering sun, and I knew the loon was returned to Crooked Lake to flush out its mate. The wet Petosky stones chattered under my boot heels so I hopped up to the bordering milkweed thicket to keep quiet, dislodging turquoise pupa as I made my way through. You ever noticed, Mr. Wade, how the monarch jewels before it butterflies? The detour was good luck. A trapper forgot his catch, that or the milkweed grew over the trap and milkweed is a fast growing dogbane. Snapped between the steel jaws was a carcass, tanned out by carrion eaters and flies. The trap had rusted shut, rendering gashes in the otherwise intact and blackened skin gone spongy as mushroom spawn. The gashes made okay eyeholes.

I lay the skin on a stump. Except for a tailbone and four leg flaps, there was no telling what sort of critter it had been. I ran my penknife across each flap then pounded river rock at it until the thing tenderized sufficient to trim out a circular shape. Twisting out two holes wide enough for twine to pass through—my labors in the Onaway broom factory have rewarded me twine in supply—I held the leather to my face. But something crawled up my nostril so I tore it off. After more futzing, I got it to lie okay, if crookedy, and tied it on back of my head with the twine. Curling my hands into monster claws, I stalked through the trees. A squirrel popped off a branch at the sight of something so unnatural and sailed up the trunk. On account of the joggling eyeholes, I got a little startled, too. Damp as snow, the mask reeked, so I shoved it under my coat for later.

The sun had taken a backseat to the pines and the lake splashed with the landing of the loon, whose exact whereabouts I could not determine. Lottie's house rose up before me. Smoke swirled out the chimney. She was home. I drew out the mask and tied it on as I stomped up the porch steps, loud as you like.

From inside the house, Lottie whispered, Who is there? I answered by ramming my shoulder into the door so it flew off the hinges. From the armchair beside the fire, a piece of negligee rose up, the flames of the fire licking through the limbs. A howl cut from her throat at the sight of this masked marauder at her door. She stumbled back, head striking the mantel. I stuffed her mouth full of my hand. She bit but I drilled my fist in until she gagged and warm solids gushed through my fingers. That negligee squirmed and slithered beneath me so I punched and kneed to make it stop, red shame rising up my neck as saliva dribbled down the rim of the mask.

Okay. Stop. Stop picturing right there, Mr. Wade. Because that's all it was, fanciful thinking. But before I could make of it heads or tails or heads again, I had come upon Lottie's house for real. She was sitting the porch shelling beans into a bucket. Shelling beans, Mr. Wade! The very picture of motherhood, her nut brown hair drawn up in a bun and a print dress tucked round her knees, her calves rising out of E.Z.'s charred trail boots. At the sight of me, her big browns went wide and her hand crept to her bosom. "You gave me a start, Simpson. You did."

"Mind?" I said, toeing the top step. She smiled and nodded so I set down at her feet. No words passed between us until she reached out her hand to rub the hair on my skull.

Same color as mine, she said.

It doesn't shine like yours.

I looked back at her, and she followed the direction of my eyes and yanked her dress down over her knees.

The lights in the sky shine, Simpson, she said, not hair.

A brown bat flicked out from under the southern eave of her house, and Lottie's boot banged the bucket so it echoed on over the water.

I rose to shake out my legs. The skin from the trap slipped out from under my coat onto the wood slats of the porch, and Lottie snatched it up before I could.

Where did you find that, Simpson?

I didn't. I mean I don't know. Can't I sometimes just have something?

She turned it over and back, and in her fine hands the skin seemed devoid of fiendishness. Bet you got frogs in your pockets, she said, arrowheads, too. Just still a boy.

Then she raised her foot to show the hole in the bottom of E.Z.'s boot. Here's a use for that skin, she said with a laugh. Let's patch it.

I clasped the boot in my hand and stared down at the hole that opened up like a mouth onto the red woolen sock beneath, and my eyes pushed back further and further, past the boot to the ankle then to her bony knee and on up to her thigh and into the cave of her dress where her drawers should be. She hauled back on her knee. But I held tight to the boot heel. The beans slid off her lap. The backs of her eyes went small and bright. Her leg began to quake. She was scared. What I couldn't do.

Simpson Willis! she said. I'm not a circus you can raise my foot over my head. Why you trying to scare me?

To my surprise, she drew herself up and gently placed her hand over mine, warming it. My grip on the boot went soft. Her leg dropped back down. She took hold of my arm and rose up. Though I elbowed her, she tucked my arm in beside hers anyway.

I know I failed you, she said. Not raising you up as I ought to have done. I'm sorry, Simpson.

Lottie escorted me lakeside of the house where the night sky flushed color, which as you know, will happen when the northern lights come our way. Like a green city burning pink kindling just beyond the dense pines, the aurora borealis drenched the night sky. She stopped in her tracks, as awed as I by this evening rainbow. For a long time we stood silent, side by side, illumined.

Lottie said, E.Z. considered this spot on Crooked Lake a lodestone for all the mysteries the natural world confers upon us. He'd have liked to see this, she said but she wasn't looking at the lights. Her eyes had settled on me and our arms tucked up together.

When the sky had hit its highest pitch, I said, This, ah, ah, this view? He wants it. Lottie, Mr. Wade knows you're sitting on a fortune.

Puddingstone? She laughed. My land doesn't yield it, Simpson. The soil's too sandy for conglomerates. I know where to find a puddingstone, of course. Pretty, but not worth a prayer. If Wade were from these parts, he'd know, too.

Wade wants something, I said. I heard he'd pay a high sum to dislodge you.

That right? she said and studied me for a time then she looked back across the lake. The timber yonder? *That* has value, she said. The state of Michigan ceded the preserve to E.Z. and his kin for stewardship. E.Z. said I was never to give up this home. I never would. I was always saving it up for you, Simpson.

Without waiting for morning light, I tore back across property lines, shooing up birds like some giddy youngster. My intention was to return that contract still in its envelope to the very table in the kitchen of the clubhouse where attorney Martin had scratched your signature, Mr. Wade. However the contract would not bear my signature. No longer would I have any part of scaring Lottie off her land.

The door to the clubhouse was locked. The contract hung dumb in my hand as I tried to work out what to do with it. Only you and your attorney Martin had come up north to vacation at your cottage homes this week. Only you would have keys. I knew this for certain or else would not have considered leaving the contract. Slipping it under the front door was what I arrived at and as I bent down to guide the envelope through the crack, the door shuddered against my shoulder. Something on the other side was pumping it like a heart. The robins startled and winged it into the trees. Why would anyone of your ilk be awake so early? The pumping stopped, so I got down to my hands and knees and set my cheek against the warm slate and looked in the crack. Directly on the other side a pair of white linen trousers bunched round a man's alligator shoe. The other foot was missing a shoe, and the hairs curled over the lip of the silk sock, like a moustache in need of primping. *HW* was stitched on the sock, Mr. Wade, Mr. *Henry Wade*. I was about to call to you when another pair of shoes came up, and a man spoke so soft on the other side.

If I had to place it in your hands, that contract was going back to you. But was the other individual with you trustworthy? What if it wasn't Martin? The only window in that stinking clubhouse was over the sink. Perhaps it would afford a better view of who else was there. But, as you know, the window's grimed up pretty good. All I could make out was that long-barreled carbine rifle you said you got over in Germany. It stood upright against the far wall by the kitchen door as if guarding the narrow weather entrance from which the back of a man in a white shirt kept appearing and disappearing, the motion something like rowing a boat. The pumping against the door had started again but the proceedings were no more intelligible from here.

I rattled up the window, intending to drop the contract into the sink. The window going up had failed to get your attention apparently. You remained tucked out of site.

The predicament was more peculiar by the minute. Whatever the two of you were at refused shape in my mind. Perhaps on account of the giddiness that had come over me since departing from Lottie.

The only practical thing was to climb through the window and deliver the contract. This was not something you'd want lying about. With one leg still dangling out the window, I remembered the mask. Wouldn't it be funny to put it on? Funny like the two of you scuffling in there like boys with a secret. Since I didn't use the mask on Lottie, why not give you a little fun for your money? I put it on.

A giggle rose up in my throat as I tied it on back of my head, one foot propped now against the sink, and it must have sounded queer or even eerie, the giggling under a mask. Something got your attention and drove you out from your little hider place, scrambling for your rifle. You pivoted round and raised the barrel to shoot but lowered it again to gape at me. Your face twisted up in fear. Or was it confusion? If it had been recognition, I reckon you'd have told me to wipe that smile off my face. I can't honestly say I was studying your expression, Mr. Wade. The entire rest of you had my attention—one sock and a white shirt was all you had on now, your knees shone red, the hair nesting about your thighs, your Johnson raised between the flaps of your shirt, like a broomstick in want of plaiting. You sighted the gun on me. If the pants around his ankles hadn't tripped him, Mr. Martin might have prevented the damage. He only managed to knock the rifle sideways. Not enough to prevent the bullet from striking my knee and breaking it to bits.

Mr. Wade, there's some who would say that what you and Mr. Martin were at was against nature. It's to those good folk I intend to appeal. 'I, Simpson Willis, agree to secure the permanent evacuation of Mrs. Lottie Ulrich from her residence, which shall be known here as 1555 Crooked Lake Lane, by any means at my disposal, for which services Mr. Harry Wade will compensate the amount of one-thousand dollars.' If you're wondering how I got it verbatim, Mr. Wade, it's because I still have the contract. More than that, I know why you hired me for the job, and it's got as much to do with the view of Crooked Lake as the Northern Lights have to do with a pot of gold. E.Z. Ulrich could have told you about the state of Michigan entrusting him with its trees if you hadn't sliced a bottle into his head. Yes, Mr. Wade, even one such as I can tell when a man's been murdered. But maybe I'm wrong. Maybe you did permit E.Z. to tell you, just didn't like what he said. Or didn't understand it. What would you know of land that holds mysteries you will never lay your hands on? What you and Mr. Martin are at is indeed against nature. But not of the kind you two were doing that morning in the clubhouse. I am not one to talk when it comes to affection held in secret, except to observe that the secret pollutes much in its path. It's the cheating, Mr. Wade, not just a poor widow out of her land, but cheating the land itself in its offices as retainer of mysteries.

If I do not get my money, I will nail the contract, along with this exact description of events as I witnessed them, leaving nothing out, to the door of the broom factory. Everyone who's anyone in Onaway will see it. They will know your secret, Mr. Wade. If I can't shame you, being a bachelor, I know your attorney friend will feel different.

Not Respectfully Yours,

Simpson Willis

Translation Folio

CHRISTINA HESSELHOLDT

Translator's Introduction

Roger Greenwald

THE DANISH WRITER CHRISTINA HESSELHOLDT (born 1962) studied at the Writers School in Copenhagen, where she has also taught for many years. Her early writing experimented with minimalism and the so-called pointillist novel. Her first significant work is a trilogy of novels that barely total 200 pages in all but are dense with many possible meanings delivered in an understated style. In 2003, she published the novel *You, My You*, an exploration of the nature of love; in 2005, the short story collection *An Endless Garden*; and in 2007, the novel *In the Bosom of the Family*, which won two major literary awards in Denmark. Her four most recent works form a cycle of linked stories: *Camilla and the Horse* (2008), *Camilla—and the Rest of the Party* (2010), *The Party Breaks Up* (2012), and *Marooned* (2014).

The Camilla cycle has elicited the highest possible praise from Danish critics. Far from being understated, this work has been described as follows by Lars Bukdahl: "There's this wild freedom and impulsiveness in her forward charge, as if she could write marvelously and in her own special style about *absolutely anything!*" A reviewer in the daily *Berlingske Tidende* declared: "Humor and grief go hand in hand, and the language shimmers from the drily caustic to the tenderly casual to the breathtakingly erotic." Torben Wendelboe commented on the cycle: "[I]t is the language—this never entirely safe language, this constantly challenging and crackling language with its lurches, sudden stops, and somersaults—that has made it such a fantastic experience to follow this cycle of stories. . . . There is no better writing in Danish."

The present story, "So Let's Talk about Flowers," is the second one in the first book in the cycle, *Camilla and the Horse* (the Danish book bears that English title). The initial name in square brackets (Camilla) indicates which character narrates this story. Since the entire cycle of stories is about the same group of friends, there are of course cross-references among the stories that can't be spotted when one reads one piece on its own. For example, in this story, when Camilla says "Memory arrives, you know on which platform," she is referring to a line in the preceding story: "A memory arrives, on Platform Cortex, as somber as a freight train." Further, a story that ends, as this one does, on an ellipsis, will not seem to break off quite so abruptly when the reader can turn immediately to the next story in the cycle. Nonetheless, each story can be enjoyed on its own, especially when we come to accept and appreciate that Hesselholdt's associative detours have their own inner logic and inevitably arrive at a destination, however unexpected.

CHRISTINA HESSELHOLDT

So Let's Talk about Flowers

[CAMILLA]

CHARLES AND I BELONG to that minority of people who were about a day late in discovering what had happened on September 11th. This was due to a combination of a language barrier, our falling in love all over again, and ordinary distraction. We were in Lisbon and were staying at the seediest hotel you can imagine. The corridors, whose carpet runners were soaked with damp and obviously placed so as to hide spots with missing floorboards, were full of trash that had never been cleared away. Worn-out furniture was piled up: beds that had been slept to death, chairs sat on to pieces, tables with thumb-shaped grooves left by melancholics who had walked, and perhaps thought, in circles, going around the tables again and again. Outside our door stood an old typewriter. When you pressed down on a key, that letter's thin metal arm was left hanging in midair, halfway between the ribbon and the other letters (the flower meadow of ancient letters), as if it wanted to say: No, I'm not doing it alone.

Who can declare he is without a certain weakness for typewriters? Each time I came back, each time I was going out, I pressed down a key. I simply couldn't resist. Like someone who sees a piano and *must* play. Memory arrives, you know on which platform: before I had written a word, let alone a poem—I was probably nineteen—I dragged my sixteen-pound typewriter with me on a train trip of many stages, to Rome, Florence, Venice, without at any time managing to write a word, but this more than paid off when a young American woman said to me that she could well understand why I was dragging the heavy beast around, "because what's an author without her typewriter?" And I was hooked. Memory given the all-clear whistle. It leaves behind a pleasant tingle, but also a flat taste in the mouth, because nothing much ever came of it. I'm like the key, dangling between heaven and earth: No, I'm not doing it alone. But I can still be fond of typewriters. And I can enjoy reading Charles's restaurant reviews and suggesting a change here and there. The reviewer's reviewer, that's me.

It wasn't only the memory of the American woman's phrase that set me tingling. Florence, New Year's Eve, a quarter of a century ago; she had long black hair and a red duffle coat with toggles, like Paddington, and maybe that was why I thought of her as a little bear, I've never been able to resist that kind of button / in that kind of duffle, / wooden and oblong, / sitting in loops.

Back to Lisbon. Our hotel room was blotchy with damp, like the rest of the hotel. When I put the plug of my hair dryer into the outlet, I could turn the light in the room on and off *with* my hair dryer; on the other hand, I couldn't get it to blow air. And then there was a mirror in which we could just barely glimpse ourselves and each other—naked and embracing each other we performed, Charles and Camilla, suitably enhanced, little more than outlines, somewhere far inside the mirror's rusty night, while (since we were doing it all the time, we were no doubt also doing it while) the airplanes flew into the towers. Afterwards, hungry from all that lovemaking, we left the room, I pressed a key down as usual, perhaps that day a *d* for disaster, and we walked with our arms around each other, hungry and happy, along the dangerous corridor and down the dangerous stairs, since the elevator was simply *too* dangerous, even for soldiers of fortune like us. Down at the front desk one of the Indian owners popped out of his room under the stairs and said something to Charles, taking him by the arm. He allowed himself to be pulled into the room. And I went along like a second fiddle. The Indian was obviously very agitated about something on the TV. I could see lots of smoke and figured it was a forest fire.

"No, we don't feel like watching a film now," Charles said in a friendly way, for he's always friendly, and drew his arm back.

"It's not a film," I said, "I think his native country's forests are burning."

"There, there," Charles said. He leaned forward, and stroking the Indian on the cheek, "I'm sure everything will be all right in the end."

The Indian understood nothing. Finally he let us go with a shrug. And without knowing it, we walked out into a changed world. But you do that all the time, of course. I hesitate to overestimate the event's importance; so many other terrible things have happened both before and since, and our countries would perhaps have closed in on us in any case. And perhaps we would have closed in on ourselves out of fear in any case. The collapse of the towers was perhaps just a trigger. Charles, for example, thinks that. Unfortunately I'm not in a position to present an independent and original political analysis; I don't have the background for it; so I rely on and repeat what I've heard and read. It's good that I have my newspaper. It's good that I have Žižek. And not least, it's good that I have Charles. And it's also good that I have Alwilda. She's sharp.

One day as I was riding along on my bike, I was stopped by a TV reporter who said would I mind if he asked me why I was using a bicycle helmet. Could there be a whole lot of answers to that question? But to surprise him I said it was because I was afraid something might fall on my head. "From above?" he asked. "From above," I repeated. "I belong to a nation of wusses who've grown afraid of everything."

"Can't you manage to speak just for yourself?" he said.

"Sure," I said, "in fact that's what I'd prefer. And long before the 11th I had started to fear the worst. Always. The only thing I'm not afraid of is salmonella. I eat raw eggs with total abandon."

"I'm hearing and writing total abandon," he said, "but we're not going to talk about eggs. Although an egg that lands on the kitchen floor and a head that lands on asphalt can obviously be compared."

And then he was suddenly in a great hurry, because he'd gotten the idea that his little feature on bicycle helmets could be introduced by a slow-motion shot of an egg smashing on a hard surface. How he ran. So no one would steal his great idea.

So let's talk about flowers, I say now (the reporter is gone). I'm sitting right now in front of a bouquet of almost black-red gladioli, at home in our living room, and thinking about what it would be like to wander into such a velvet funnel. Now don't imagine this is about a woman's sex; beware, for this deals once again with death. To wander into a funnel of velvet like this one, turn your head, and see it close up behind you. To be surrounded, locked in, suffocated in delicious fragrance, pressed against soft walls, and to have to die the flower-death.

But where does it come from, I ask myself—and it happens that Alwilda asks me, and Charles too—this orbiting around death. For a long time I owed them an answer. I shrugged and turned my face away and resolved that in the future I would keep death to myself. As if it were only my problem, mine and mine alone. So I was happy when one day, in V. S. Naipaul's *The Enigma of Arrival*, I found a possible answer.

I learned the passage by heart, and the next time Alwilda asked me, I replied, "To see the possibility, the certainty, of ruin, even at the moment of creation: it was my temperament. Those nerves had been given me as a child in Trinidad partly by our family's circumstances: the half-ruined or broken-down houses we lived in, our many moves, our general uncertainty. . . ."

"Trinidad," said Alwilda in disbelief. "But we lived in Roskilde the whole time, and your place there was perfectly nice, not at all broken down."

"Insecurity," I said somberly, "insecurity: the furniture was moved around a bit, I was farmed out to relatives for long stretches, there was a lot of sickness, my life got turned upside down suddenly, people arrived and departed."

"Yeah, childhood's a quagmire," Alwilda said, "you get stuck in it. Every single day I stupidly repeat what others have said to me. Who's talking through me now, I ask myself, is it little Mama or little Grandpa, who was it again who was utterly disgusted by a spiderweb on his broom, who was it that yelled at me when I had swept the webs off the high ceilings and had forgotten to clean the broom, and there was something on the bristles that looked like moldy porridge. And now it's me. I don't care what the broom looks like. But a yell comes out of me. When Daniel hasn't cleaned it after he's used it."

"Isn't it a bit too easy to fall back on the notion that someone's speaking through you? Shouldn't a person take responsibility for what he says?"

"But when you *are* being spoken through. First I had to have thick enough—what is it, again?—thick enough hide to put up with my grandpa yelling at me. And then when I'm yelled through, I'm supposed to be responsible for that?"

"At least you get the satisfaction of yelling at Daniel."

"Who will later yell the same thing at a new person, who in turn will yell it. . . ."

Translated from the Danish by Roger Greenwald

TONY HOAGLAND

Economica

The waiter in the expensive restaurant
gets tipped nine dollars for pouring a glass of wine.
The waitress in the hash joint
gets a dollar twenty-five for delivering

three plates of scrambled eggs with hash browns,
toast, Canadian bacon, biscuits and gravy,
plus medium OJs for two and coffee for everyone.

This is the condition of which Marx spoke,
which has forged the deformed world,
to which you are obedient,

—as the bill arrives,
and the credit card is signed and run,
and the receipt sticks out its little tongue

and you feel that small frisson which comes
from being ever so much on top of it—
as in the foyer of the restaurant, Andre

wishes you a very good evening sir, indeed,
and clicks his heels;
as in the diner, with no one watching,

the waitress scrubs at a stain on the tabletop
and laughs at something
nobody hears but her.

Exodus

So I clambered over the chain link fence
and walked down to the high school playing fields,

past the big roll of Astroturf beside the stadium,
waiting to be unfurled;

and last year's scoreboard that still says
Rattlesnakes 7, Visitors 19.

Walked under the bleachers and around the circular track
where the automatic sprinklers, rain or shine, go on,

and the little tufts of weed
pop up their raggedy bouquets of faded lavender and blue.

Clouds in the west, above the old brick gym,
and a breeze that ripples through the ivy

like a sleeve, which shimmers,
as if it was proud of being green.

All my life,
I have been held up by water,

loved by women,
ignored by war.

Why then do I mutter to myself while walking?
and glare at the tops of my shoes,

as if I was standing on a cliff,
or at the railing of a bridge,

ready to leap down again
into the raging river of childhood?

ED SKOOG

Run the Red Lights

When my mother sent me for cigarettes I'd buy
a candy bar too, sign her name to the book
and walk out with the green and white carton,
Virginia Slims 100s, under my arm,
the chocolate already gone. Sugar, my god!
like newspaper cartoon panels spread out
on the kitchen table where I'd pretend to smoke,
a little imitation of my mother.
After the corner store closed we made our groceries
at Dillons, joined the impersonal. A villain
snatched her purse there when I was away at college
and on the phone she told me, excitedly,
how Topeka police chased the culprit, and she named
each street, each intersection and landmark,
the whole adventure, just for her.
I'm grateful now for that sedentary house
though I've grown as large on candy as John Candy.
My older brothers left home and our meals stayed
the same, a skillet high with beef stroganoff,
pot roast in broth, chili con carne,
cheese sandwiches with mayo, flocks of fried chicken.
Then the whole house went on a diet of cold
tofu cubes, a broken disc of lemon in a water glass,
cottage cheese measured onto lettuce,
and then back to London broil the next night,
no questions asked—lovely. We were emotions
without form, and I carry it with me,
not just in frame, arm and jowl and belly,
but here in the intergalactic space of written
thought, the infinite stage where we come
talk to each other. Sugar makes me curious.
After Katrina, I took the diet where you eat meat,
and lost almost a hundred pounds from a surfeit

of bacon, sautéed pork medallions, beef & lamb.
The weight fell away like a knight's armor
after a joust. I bought shirts at a regular store.
I played softball and ran bases, bounded them,
as if on a new, more forgiving planet. And
I went crazy, evened out, broke down again,
inconsolable at the finale of *Six Feet Under*,
tears for my mother, postponed, and more
torrented for delay. Opening the book of grief
requires that you read all the way to the end,
every time. Driving to work, I stopped
bewildered at a gas station, paid cash for two
Snickers that provided more salvation
than I have ever known from religion's acres.
I write about the West and the South and home
their tenderness and trouble and the weird spirits
that brake the best days. Still I find myself down
by the river at twilight despite the stories
of jaguars under the bridge. All day was interview
where the jaguars were questions. On the bridge
deliberate-seeming people walk by like victorious aliens,
past the consequential palaces lit as before, the faces
turning in their rotisseries. It is like waking a sleeper
in his illness. Deer tracks through downtown snow;
industry and highway puff the unappeasable whiteness,
unappeasable and motherly, ash from midnight cigarettes.
My mother looked a little bit like Alex Chilton,
lead singer of the Box Tops, and then the greatest
rock band of all time, Big Star, and a solo career.
My mother had a solo career, playing solitaire
and watching her own TV in the kitchen, and dying
before everyone else. I used to see Chilton often
around New Orleans, in line at the grocery store,
walking down Esplanade Avenue, and on stage.
Dying, he urged his wife to run the red lights
—his last words—and when I had to leave
my mother in the hospital that was hard
and then again at the funeral home I set
a marble under her folded hands, don't know
why. It's been ten years. Ten fingers, the

closed eye of each knuckle, each nail
its years' fullest day moon. Which of us
shed the other? The scar from opening a window,
such force to move the wood frame, so little
to shatter the glass it held. To be held like that
again. Ten years, so forty seasons, eighty
endings and beginnings, well, always a little
gust in them which is the sigh of how
she would note leaf and bird, porch shadows.
One hand to hold the coffee cup, one the cigarette.
The red ember she became at midnight. Red light. Eye.

ROGER GREENWALD

Norway

Norway is my grandmother's house,
though she never lived here.
These wooden floors, plaster moldings
are hers, though she did not have them.
She sat by these ripply windows
when I left and when I came back,
waving in both directions.
Her kitchen was not like Norway
but she is here in the sound of a wood board
hung by its hole on a wood peg.
Norwegian is her language
though she did not speak it. I hear her
in the rise and the tone-fall.
Norway is her granite, and her hands
warm under the blanket
to see if my feet are too cold for sleep.
Norway is the comforter she never owned,
in a white cotton sleeve as smooth as her arm.
Norway is the nameless country she left.
The landscape of names I return to.

LINDSEY DRAGER

To Possess Is to Extinguish: A Gothic Essay

MY LIBRARY IS AN AERIAL graveyard. There are dead birds lining the outside perimeter on the cement window sills on all seven floors. In the winter they get buried under the snow that gathers on the overhang. Then in spring there are perfectly preserved birds that appear from beneath the melting snow and I can count how many were collected by the wide transparency of the window during the winter months.

My mother's ring finger is deformed in such a way that it is impossible for her to wear her wedding band. She was born with an underdeveloped knuckle so that when she makes a fist, there is a shallow dip instead of a hump under the stretched white skin on the third finger of her left hand. She used to wear the ring on a chain to pledge her allegiance to my father, but now claims her claustrophobia prevents her from wearing necklaces.

My father is the president of his own company. All the men I date look like him.

My mother gave me a deck of Tarot cards as a gift when I moved into my first apartment. She said I didn't need to learn how to use the cards, told me just to be sure that I wrapped them in a pretty velvet cloth and pulled them out only when I was drinking Merlot. She said to use a lot of candles when I was reading someone's Tarot. "But Mom, should I really be screwing with the cosmos?" I asked her. And for the first time in longer than I could remember, she didn't answer my question.

My fish Mort will die the day I turn twenty. I will be wary to leave him alone in my apartment for the extended weekend, so I'll put him in a mason jar and kept him in the cup compartment of my truck for the duration of the four-hour ride home. When I pull out of the parking lot of the complex he will be fine. It won't be until exit 56 of U.S. 23 that I will look down to check on him and see that he is floating upside down.

My neighbor from New Mexico asks me to read him his Tarot the first time we meet. I had read almost everyone's Tarot that night and he is one of the last. He knocks on my door and I tell him to come in. I am sitting cross-legged on the floor and only three candles illuminate the room as all the lights are off. We both hold a glass of Merlot, his less full than mine. I tell him to shuffle the cards and cut the deck. He clears his throat, shuffles quietly and then I flip a card over. It is a dead bird. Though I did not know how to read the cards, I tell my neighbor from New Mexico that the Tarot says his current relationship is in trouble. He says this is impossible and gives me a drunken grin. I say the Tarot does not lie. He notes that he and his girlfriend will be married and gives me a drunken grin. I ask him to hold out his hand so that I might inspect his knuckles. His fingers are very dark and slender, damp and cold. We debate about the validity of the Tarot before others who want their reading knock on my door. Before he leaves, my neighbor from New Mexico grins again and touches the freckle on the left side of my face, just above my lip. "Nice to meet you," he says.

My mother collects the little weapons from games of Clue. We are required to buy the game at the Salvation Army, Goodwill, rummage or garage sales if it has been priced at fewer than two dollars. If it has been priced at greater than two dollars, we are required to haggle.

My library has seven floors, two of which contain volumes of academic journals. On these floors exclusively there are pillars on top of which dictionaries are placed. On the day before my twentieth birthday I enter the library and head up to floor four. I walk to one of the dictionaries to look up an unfamiliar word that was used in my last class. The word is *exacerbescence*. In flipping the pages, however, I pause on the term execute, which someone has underlined with pencil. I read the definition of the word, which means "a carrying out or putting into effect" as well as "a prescription for death or assassination." I read the definition again to be sure I have fully comprehended the word. When I finish reading the entire definition I realize that *execute* means both to initiate and to end. I forget the word I started to look up and reread this definition. I put my finger under the text and drag it back and forth. I press too hard and smear the ink. I finish reading. I read again.

My neighbor from New Mexico uses numbers to find order in the world. He believes in objectivity and class. Once when we were lying in bed he grabbed a pen that was sitting on my side table and started writing on my forearm, the wet ink drying instantly in the dark. When I woke up the next morning I inspected my arm in the light and found that he had written out Pythagorean's Theorem. I copied the equation onto a piece of notebook paper and when he woke up he asked what I was doing. I looked at him, his hair wild and his eyes closed, the voice escaping him low. I watched him for a moment before I responded. Then he readjusted my pillow and told me to come back to bed.

My roommate the photo minor wakes me up at 2 AM. She wants me to help with her current project, which is supposed to be a photo essay. She wants me to light a candle and then blow it out. I do this and she takes a number of photos of me throughout the process; a photo of me scratching the match head against the sandpaper, a photo of me touching the flame to the wick, a photo of me opening my mouth to breathe in the air that will be used to exterminate the flame. When I am done this first time, she tells me to do it again. I light the candle and blow it out, light the candle and blow it out. At 2:45 AM she grabs a beer from the fridge and we break before starting again. I light her candle. I blow it out.

My professor tells us that because the gothic tradition is concerned primarily with anxiety, it is always gesturing toward a future tense to speculate and project on what might be, rather than hover in the space of what is. This anxiety about a future is further complicated in American Gothic, where the installation of national narratives like manifest destiny or the American dream underscore that the power of identity relies more on a future than on a history. While these ideologies do not always necessarily direct us forward but rather West and up respectively, they implicitly argue against looking back. It is for this reason that American Gothic seems concerned with the spectral and kinetic space of the imminent, made manifest through progeny. Indeed, the ghosting that happens in American Gothic tales finds itself performing this anxiety about the future both in plot with its consistent motif of transgressive domestic desire, but also through narrative mode in its use of prolepsis and manipulation of past progressive and future tense.

My mother will call me the morning I turn twenty to tell me that a pheasant has crashed through the window in the sunroom. She will be crying in a very frantic way that I haven't heard in a long while. Her voice will bring back sad memories of my childhood. I will tell her that it is okay and that she should simply shut the sun room door and deal with the pheasant tomorrow. But she'll say that there are bloody feathers everywhere and the bird is still moving and there are shards of glass inside its back she doesn't know what to do. In a very soft voice I will tell her to shut the door. I will hear the sliding glass that connects the living room to the sunroom close very slowly. Then we won't speak for a long time. I'll listen to my mother's breathing become less and less frenzied through the mouth of the phone. Finally she will give a little sigh and say, "It stopped moving."

My library provides a copy of *Science News* which I pick up one afternoon after counting dead birds. I read on the cover that a five-hundred-year-old math problem has recently been solved in Japan. The problem was solved when a mathematician halfway across the world discovered that a shape dubbed E8 had 243 degrees. "The degrees work in a funnel form and the shape looks like a kaleidoscope," the man said. In the interview, the journalist suggests that we live in a three dimensional world and that

243 is a large number in comparison. In response, the article says the mathematician laughed. "You should think of the dimensions as degrees of freedom," the mathematician said.

My professor is not mine; he belongs to the university, like my library.

My roommate the photo minor will get a call the evening I turn twenty; my broken voice describing Mort's demise. After I leave her the voicemail I will enter my kitchen where my mother has placed Mort on the counter with nothing underneath; just Mort's sad orange body on top of naked Formica. When I ask her what she is doing, she'll turn around so I can see she's cleaning out the mason jar that served as Mort's tomb. Then I'll hear her voice tell me that her can of metal weapons from games of Clue is overflowing and I wouldn't mind if she used this one, would I?

My neighbor from New Mexico has a steady girlfriend from high school. He will knock on my door the night before I turn twenty when all my roommates and I are watching a *Twilight Zone* marathon. He will sit on the floor and produce a can of beer from his blazer. As he cracks it open, my roommate the philosophy minor will go upstairs to bed. When the first episode ends, he will pull a second beer from his other blazer pocket. After a while I'll stretch out on the couch and my roommate the photography minor will tell us goodnight and head up to bed. When my neighbor hears her door shut, he will scoot across the floor to where I am lying on the couch. As another episode ends, he'll stand up. I will think he is leaving. But instead he'll take off his blazer and tell me to scoot over. I'll sit up on the couch and he'll lie down with his head in my lap. I will stroke his hair for a while before I realize he is crying. For a long time we'll stay that way. Then I will say, "You look like my father."

My library tells me in a textbook I borrow that ninety percent of marriages in which one spouse suffers from mental illness fail.

My mother and my father will not last.

My neighbor from New Mexico will ask me to go with him to help pick out his first pair of glasses the day before I turn twenty. In the car he'll talk a lot about the films he's just watched and about how his classes are harder than mine because the humanities are for the soft. When we get to the optometrist's, we'll notice that the house across the street bears a neon signs in all the windows that have the day's date written across them in thick black sharpie. There is a demolition truck parked in the front yard, but no people around. We will spend forty minutes choosing a pair of two hundred dollar glasses that he feels ambivalent about. On our way outside I will ask him how his girlfriend is. He won't look at me when he says they are engaged. Just as I am offering my congratulations, we will exit to face a pile of house that had stood erect just forty minutes prior. We will stand still for a moment looking at the domestic litter before I sigh loudly and start walking to his car.

My mother tells me that New Mexico is known as the land of enchantment.

My professor tells us that American Gothic asks these questions: Does the past end? Does it persist? If so, how?

My neighbor from New Mexico will send me an electronic message the morning after his divorce. *The papers are signed and I see you have become someone*, it will read. I will think of the wine and the birds, my professor and the weapons. I will think of my mother's knuckle and the Tarot cards that are missing in the catalog of my memory and how everything that is lost is just somewhere else. I will call the photo minor and I will want to ask her about our night with her candles but I will not, because not knowing is safer. Just as I am ready to apologize again for Mort, this emblem of our shared life so many years ago, she will tell me that she is with child and that by some miracle of the cosmos she is carrying two. I will draw my hand across the spines of the books on my shelf and think she is producing an archive. I will work very hard not to think of my father and my voice will smile and I will say "My, my."

Translation Folio

THREE URUGUAYAN POETS

Introduction

Jesse Lee Kercheval

WHEN U.S. TREASURY SECRETARY JACK Lew announced a plan to put a woman on ten dollar bills to be issued in 2020, the 100th anniversary of the 19th amendment, I couldn't help pointing out to friends that Uruguay already has a woman on their $1000 peso note. And that woman is a poet, Juana de Ibarbourou (1892-1979), one of the most popular poets in South America. Uruguay is a small country, just 3.3 million people. But it has produced a long line of strong women poets stretching from Juana de Ibarbourou and Delmira Agustini (1886-1914) to Amanda Berenguer (1921-2010). Idea Vilariño (1920-2009) formed part of the famed Uruguayan literary Generation of '45 along with such writers as Juan Carlos Onetti, Mario Benedetti and ex-officio Argentine member Jorge Luis Borges. The three poets presented here, Circe Maia, Laura Cesarco Eglin, and Karen Wild, are living representatives of this unbroken tradition of Uruguayan women's voices.

At 83, Circe Maia, born in Montevideo, Uruguay, in 1932, belongs to the generation just after the Generation of '45. Circe's father had her first book of poems, *Plumitas*, published in 1944 when she was only eleven years old. *En el tiempo*, her first book written as an adult, was published in 1958 and her tenth, *Dualidades*, was published in 2014. Though born in Montevideo, Maia has lived most of her life in the northern city of Tacuarembó, where she taught philosophy, a required subject in Uruguayan high schools, to generations of students. In 1972, when the military dictatorship took power in Uruguay, military police broke into Maia's house in the middle of the night and arrested her physician husband for supporting the Movimiento de Liberación Nacional-Tupamaros (MLN-T), leaving Maia behind only because she had just given birth to their youngest daughter. She wrote of this experience in her autobiographical novel *Un Viaje a Salto*, published in a bilingual edition in the United States as *A Trip to Salto*. Because of this, an Uruguayan reading her work would be quick to sense an undercurrent in a poem like "Signs": "Question marks / Barbs / of interrogation / like fish-hooks / go and return empty." But in the poem's ending, she is the philosophy teacher, "Let them go. / The water, the air itself, / and even the light, / are clear / answers / to other signs."

Laura Cesarco Eglin was born in Montevideo in 1976. She is the author of three poetry collections, *Llamar al agua por su nombre*, *Sastrería* and *Los brazos del saguaro*. She holds a master's degree in English from the Hebrew University of Jerusalem and an MFA in Creative Writing from the University of Texas at El Paso. She cites Idea Vilariño, one of the poets of the Generation of '45, as one of her favorite Uruguayan poets. Vilariño is best known for her intense, confessional love poems addressed to novelist Juan Carlos Ontetti, and Cesarco Eglin's poems are more personal, more conversational in tone than Maia's. Her poem "Agency" starts with a direct, but intimate voice, "I don't need a kaleidoscope when I can / lie down and close my eyes." But her maternal grandparents were Holocaust survivors who came to Uruguay as refugees after WWII and, as in Maia's poems, the reader can feel the weight of history in Cesarco Eglin's prose poem about her grandmother, "Photogenic": "When I look at the photo we are there, as is her shaved head. A flash in the eyes is a flashback in her history. It hurts. Persists."

Karen Wild was born in Montevideo in 1984. Like Cesarco Eglin, she has been able to study abroad, at the University of Paris. She is now an assistant professor at the Universidad de la República. Her book of poetry *Anti-Férula* is forthcoming in English from Toad Press as *Anti-Ferule*. At 31, she is belongs fully to the generation of Uruguayan poets raised in the post-dictatorship era of democracy and boom-and-bust capitalism, but she lists as her favorite a poet of Maia's generation, the marvelously strange Marosa Di Giorgio (1932-2004). The opening to Wild's poem "Thread of Blood in the Sky" shows more than a touch of di Giorgio's surrealism: "In the sky a thread of blood / Like a stream on a map, / like a stream of a continent on a map." But in the poem's last lines, there are also echoes of Maia's clean, spare language and philosophic approach "Look / You shall not hope for anything / to happen. Nothing / No desire to fall: it's in your blood / Do not."

In addition to Juana de Ibarbourou place on the 1000 peso note, her home in Melo, Uruguay, is a museum and cultural center. I have been there and seen the "room of her own" where she wrote. I have made the pilgrimage to Tacuarembó, a five-hour bus trip from Montevideo, to visit Circe Maia in her home. At poetry events in Montevideo, when I sit and listen to the more established poets such as Tatiana Oroño and Silvia Guerra read with young poets, often still students, I see this strong poetic tradition being passed, hand to hand, poet to poet, and it moves me deeply. I hope you will feel the same reading these poems.

CIRCE MAIA : Three Poems

Yesterday, A Eucalyptus

A cold branch turns to the East
—the one that has new leaves—
but the trunk, which faces the setting sun,
is warm to the touch of the hand,
warm and smooth—surprisingly smooth—
like porcelain, not wood.

(Clearly a porcelain which might have held
hot tea inside, that the hand enjoyed, until it cooled)

The color . . . impossible
to define: a shade
between gray and pink, on the green background.
No, you don't see it, can't even imagine it.

Its being is memory. Unattainable
by other thoughts. Not one idea
touches it . . . What should we say
about that touch and the warmth of that trunk?

Only the skin, the palm of the hand,
in some way saves it, at least.

October Rain

The drops touch the tiles with such smoothness
that it does not appear very real, this rain.
No noise.
It seems to turn on, then off, the small circles
hitting the water, softly.

They blink on, blink off, like small signals
—changeable, superfast—
a secret code.

Signs

Question marks
barbs
of interrogation
like fish-hooks
go and return empty.

Let them go.

The water, the air itself,
and even the light,
are clear
answers
to other signs.

Translated from the Spanish by Jesse Lee Kercheval

Downpour

A gray sky's anxiety
knotted with the timbre of clouds
unloading itself in buckets to recycle the sea
to free itself from the urge to peel back
screams, to leave them naked
in hoarse thunderclaps and lightning
the sea keeps licking the sand
to shape it more than the wind
the steps that leave their prints
are erased, disappearing
like they disappeared you
leaving me with one less fingerprint
with each question that I refused to answer
while today the grayness swells
over the weeping, thundering its images
its electric shock after shock is
what remains of you.

Agency

I don't need a kaleidoscope when I can
lie down and close my eyes, my gaze fixed
on a window and my breathing arming the wavering
of the light, arming what I will not name, will not give
stillness, so that it happens in spite of me
although I know that when the mountain melts
and the cork branches out, I will be in Portugal; the wind
gusts to its side, leaves loosen themselves, some
underneath this pen also indicate the course
of the current today without needing to wet the tip
of the finger to feel where it comes from,
I don't see it coming; it's here, time's ventriloquist
says that I say that it says that I say
I say

Photogenic

I

She turns around and doesn't look at the camera. She looks at us. She leaves the frame. She brings us, little by little, on by one, together. The photo, without her. She takes from us what comes from others. Those features that reveal the ones she lost in the war. To take a photo is to resist remembrance. To look at a photo while it's being taken is to help her recover the memory.

II

She would find herself in the photo. In the one of her family that she wanted to show me. To show me in order to recognize herself. If she doesn't come through in this photo maybe she'll return with those who aren't here. If she looks at us, maybe she'll see them. If again she finds that place on the border of the frame, they will also see us. That place in the eye, with which one sees what is faint, is precisely between the two photos. She knows that she has to see if it can be done; to disrupt the development, to return the third person plural to the intimacy of the first person, plural, singular.

III

When I look at the photo we are there, as is her shaved head. A flash in the eyes is a flashback in her history. It hurts. Persists. She attaches herself to abandonment—to being the only survivor in the family. She looks at us in order to be kept company. She doesn't look to overcome the forever or afterward. If she would look at the camera, it would capture the fractions of her that remain.

Translated from the Spanish by Lauren Shapiro

KAREN WILD : Three Poems

Thread of Blood in the Sky

In the sky a thread of blood
Like a stream on a map,
like a stream of a continent on a map

The map is in the sky
and we bend our necks back to see

The map is in the sky
and is unreachable as the map
The map seems reachable
but is not enough to be tangible to be
The map, nonetheless, is
but so unreachable

So the sky has a thread

Wants not to fall from nothing. Wants to live
Wants not to fall nonetheless. There is no

certainty it will appear
They say the sky will not fall on our head
will not fall is what they say

When the threads fall in torment,
how surely they fall and torment,

we must remain standing

When the blood falls on us

Wanting, wanting, To make something of the blood
but something that is not anything
Wanting, wanting, Remain standing,

neck back. When the thread of blood
falls, when in torment soaks us,
our desire shall become
an act. An unspecified act
in principle, it can be anything
but is not just anything. Something has to be done

The sky has a thread
Look
You shall not hope for anything
to happen. Nothing

No desire to fall: it's in your blood
Do not

Shelter from the Sky

She protects her head from the sky

The sky is a place way up

She rises endlessly to the sky
Walk or climb the sky is endless
She suffers because the sky is a place
she can't reach and she rises
Stops, and leans down

The sky is a place below

She furrows her brow
and pushes through a snag to rise

The path to the sky falls away in a bend
seems a surefooted place
the sky is nowhere's land

The sky is no place at all

The Sky Knows No Walls

If it is very cold
and you're out in the open
Find a wall to lean on

A wall is something very tall
After a wall another wall
that grows
Then continues on the wall
and adds more walls
Up to the sky
The sky knows no walls
She lifts her face to the sky
and leans on the walls

Always fantasizes crossing the wall
and finding on the other side
          the sky
          the water

Translated from the Spanish by Ron Paul Salutsky

DAVID MEISCHEN

The Yellow Dress

I.

DORENE PURCHASED THE FABRIC ON a rare shopping trip to Corpus Christi. Six weeks ago, she'd circled the date on her calendar. Saturday, March 8, 1958. Other purchases taken care of, she was browsing among bolts of cotton, fingering first one print and then another, when Michael tapped her at the elbow and said, "This one." He'd asked to come along as a birthday treat. The youngest of her sons, he'd been nine for all of four days. Dorene had almost forgotten he was with her. Ordinarily, when Michael had his mother to himself, he chattered nonstop. He hadn't said a word, though, since they entered the store. Colors, textures, varieties of print—cotton, linen, satin, velveteen—they seemed to put him in a trance. The bolt of fabric he wanted for her was a lovely mercerized cotton, a solid among aisles of prints, a shimmering lemony yellow.

Dorene hadn't worn anything so bright in years. She said as much.

Michael pulled the bolt of fabric and led her to a mirror.

"Look," he said, draping the loose end of the swath on her shoulder and unfurling the bolt down across her torso.

Dorene had a naturally dark complexion. On occasion, where she wasn't known, she'd been addressed in Spanish—once on her honeymoon. She'd said *No habla español* and then laughed Robert out of the ire the mistake had sparked in him. This color, though, so thick it made her think of egg yolk, this yellow glowed against her skin.

When Michael said buy it, she didn't say no. Minutes later, browsing pattern books, he tapped her again and pointed.

The dress in the color sketch was what Dorene would call a dancing dress—a full swirling skirt set off by bands of rickrack, a scoop-neck top much like a tailored peasant blouse, with elastic at neckline and sleeves. More rickrack too, circling the scoop-neck, the sleeves.

Why not? she thought. It's time.

OVER supper that evening, after Robert came in from the fields, she held back and let Michael tell about the material, the pattern he'd picked out for her. Jimmy Don, her eldest, smirked. Max, ever the instigator, made a fist and socked Michael on the arm.

"You are such a pantywaist," he said.

"Not another word," Robert answered him. "Not at this table." But the look on his face carried the same judgment.

"Apologize," Dorene said to Max.

"That's okay." Michael waved off the insult. "I don't care what he says." Excusing himself, he fetched the shopping bag from Dorene's dresser chair and, with a magician's gesture, pulled the fabric from it.

"Something bright for a change," Jimmy Don said, clapping in her direction.

"Look at what she's gonna make with it!" Michael handed the pattern to Jimmy Don.

Her eldest gave an appreciative whistle and spoke to Robert. "You'll have to step out with Momma."

"Give me that." Robert lay hold of the pattern. His face soured. "Look like a floozy wearing this thing."

In a single motion, smooth as quicksilver, Jimmy Don stood up.

"You can't talk to Momma like that," he said. "Nobody can."

"This is my house," said Robert, standing as he spoke, menace edging his voice. "I'll say whatever I goddamn please."

Dorene stood and said her husband's name. "Robert."

"Woman."

She didn't waver under his threat. She hadn't wanted this, but it was here and she wasn't afraid.

"Jimmy Don," she said.

Her son turned to her. With her eyes, she indicated his chair. Then she sat down. Jimmy Don sat down.

Robert stood for a moment longer. "Next time you go shopping," he said, "leave your boy there home with the men." Then he too sat down.

DORENE admired in Jimmy Don the calm that came over him when he sensed someone near to him was threatened. He betrayed no fear, didn't even seem angry. Only intractable. He would not back down. Robert called it disrespect—often and loudly—but his bluster was like air escaping under pressure. Harmless. Anyone could see that he admired his firstborn. Jimmy Don was the son who wouldn't be intimidated.

The confrontation at an end, Dorene put the fabric and the pattern back in the shopping bag. Michael didn't object when she put them out of sight beneath the window seat. He took it to heart, though—she could see that. It wasn't the dress that had triggered the scene at the supper table. Michael surely knew, as Robert privately confessed, that what bothered his father was the role their youngest had played.

"Max got it right," Robert told her. "The boy's going girly. You encourage it."

Michael had weathered his father's looks—he'd taken flak from his brothers—with hardly a ripple. But the scene over the yellow dress put a bit in his teeth. He avoided games and outings with his brothers, kept a rein on his enthusiasms at the supper table. On the rare occasion when he broke free of caution, he was likely to stiffen mid-gesture, as if hearing his father's voice.

THREE years passed, and then one afternoon, with an April breeze drifting into the house, Dorene raised the window seat and saw a corner of yellow fabric down among her sewing things.

She was at the table looking over the pattern, the material laid out before her, when Jimmy Don passed through. As before, he whistled.

"Do it," he said. "Daddy'll get over it."

Jimmy Don was sixteen going on thirty. He'd been fully grown at thirteen, with a man's voice that men listened to. He'd discovered himself in the mirror, regularly looked there while he smoothed the wavy black hair he'd inherited from her. The eyes, the cheekbones—he was too good looking for his own good, trailing the scent of a heavy, oily cologne wherever he went. Around his brothers, his friends, he was still the cocky prankster. But he could shed his boyish self with ease.

His *do it* was curt, hard-edged, but it was enough. Dorene arranged the sections of her pattern, pinned them into place, and got to work with her scissors. Over supper, when Robert asked about her day, she told him she'd started the dress.

Max gave her a look. Michael smiled but held his tongue.

"Get ready for a night on the town," Jimmy Don said. "Where you taking her, Daddy?"

He didn't let up until they'd settled on the last Saturday in April—a dance at the Cotton Patch. "Like old times," Jimmy Don said, his voice all mockery now, a reference to the stories she'd told her sons when they were small. They knew their father had once been more outgoing, that—especially before Robert shipped out to the South Pacific—their parents had spent many a Saturday night dancing in the open air.

Gulf breezes made the Cotton Patch the most popular dance spot in the county—a slab of cement a mile or so outside Nopalito, unroofed, with a tall picket fence in place of walls. Picnic tables and benches framed the dance floor, with tin sheds for bandstand and bar. It was a pathetic sight by daylight, with huisache and prickly pear bristling up out of hardpan, no cotton fields in sight. But when sundown came and cars drove up and people walked in and sat down and started talking and the music started up, there was nothing like it. Dorene had been happier there, without even thinking about it, than any other place her life had offered.

Afternoons, then, when she could find the time, she worked on her dress, a puzzle forming as she hummed at her Singer, a change in Jimmy Don she couldn't explain. Without notice, the humor had disappeared from his wisecrack commentary. His words were knife-sharp, his sarcasm, his judgments of others tempered by withering heat. He was especially harsh with Michael. Cupcake, he called him. Marmalade. Mr. Bubbly.

One afternoon, she walked in on them—Michael trapped between the kitchen counter and the stove, Jimmy Don waving his arms wildly, a cruel parody.

"You don't like it?" he was saying. "Learn to use 'em. Put 'em up." He hunched into a boxer's stance and made sparring motions, this time aping what his little brother might look like if he tried boxing. But Michael had a surprise in store. He made a fist and socked Jimmy Don in the gut.

During the bent-over gasping for breath that followed, Dorene stepped in.

"That's enough," she said, and when Jimmy Don threatened to throttle his little brother, she stood between them. Her power with him held. He wouldn't touch her. He wouldn't insult her by getting around her or shoving her out of the way.

"I'm used to him," is what Michael said when Jimmy Don was gone. "He's got a mean edge lately."

"Wonder what's wrong."

"You know Jimmy Don. He wouldn't tell you if you asked."

II.

JIMMY DON'S TROUBLE WAS PATSY Geistweidt—something she'd told him ten days back. A blunt, bare little sentence that had changed everything. Patsy had a dazzling temper. The fire in her, that's what he'd noticed first—it drew him in. And he'd discovered that having sex with her after one of her flare-ups—or even during—could be spectacular.

Patsy was twenty-one. What there was between them had started up last fall on the evening of her birthday, when he approached her, celebrating with friends at a dance.

"Have you even started shaving?" she said and brushed his cheek with the back of her hand.

"I've got hair where it counts."

"Well," she said, "I guess you can dance with me then."

Before the night was done, they had fucked in a cornfield. For the rest of the fall, they carried on secretly. He didn't mind staying out of sight with her. He'd been with plenty of women before Patsy, but he hadn't gone out with any of them, hadn't given them a second thought outside of arranging to bed them. Patsy changed all that. What they did when they got off alone—he liked it too much. He liked her too much. After sneaking around with her for a couple of months, he suggested public outings, but even after he turned sixteen—that was back in January—she'd been embarrassed about his age. Patsy claimed she hadn't even told her cousin Carter, and they were all but joined at the hip.

Then one night in March, she got in Jimmy Don's car and said, "Let's do something respectable." They spent the evening with Carter and Arlene, newly married. Carter would have liked Jimmy Don if he had vampire teeth and a cape. The Geistweidt cousins had been dancing partners—incurable show-offs—since Carter was six and Patsy five. They finished each other's sentences, passed a drumstick back and forth from an order of fried chicken. Whatever one did, the other approved. If you wanted Patsy in your life, you got Carter. They were a package deal. Patsy's first big blow-up at Jimmy Don had come when he'd made a wisecrack about all the time she spent dancing with someone she couldn't enjoy after.

For a month, then, in the eyes of the town, Patsy and Jimmy Don were a couple. On Friday, April 14, they had supper at Carter and Arlene's. Whiskey sours afterwards. A game of spades. Patsy had little to say during the evening; she wanted to go straight home when they were done at cards—said she was tired, didn't want to rumple her skirt. She lapsed into silence on the drive. Jimmy Don switched on the radio and whistled along. At her house, he killed the engine and cut the lights. A quiet minute with Patsy was the most he could expect. Her parents would be waiting inside; she didn't want them to fret.

When he turned to Patsy, she had turned away, her nose to the passenger window.

"I'm pregnant," she said.

For moments at a stretch, looking at the back of her head, he wondered how far the stillness reached, what had happened even to the sound of breathing.

"Well?" she said, as if to the window.

"You can't be."

"I think I'd know."

"It can't be mine."

Now she turned to face him. "You might want to think before you say another word."

"We use condoms," he said. "Every time." She'd cured him of calling them rubbers.

"One of them leaked."

"How would that happen?"

"You get pretty excited. Must've torn one."

"Look," he said. "It can't be mine."

Patsy slapped him hard, the flat of her hand connecting to bone, to the hinge in his jaw. The pain was like electricity, shooting into his nose and eyes.

He had never hit a woman. He didn't intend to now. He grabbed her hands and held them.

Patsy sucked air into her lungs and shouted. "I have a baby in me! It's yours, goddammit! You did this to me!"

A light came on at her parents' bedroom window—a minute later, the porch light too.

Patsy got out of the car and leaned into the open door. "Congratulations," she said. "You're a father." She slammed the door and was gone.

JIMMY Don was good at juggling the difficult things. He'd been playing referee at home since before he was ten, stepping between his parents when his father threatened to get out of hand. For several years already, he'd been earning money by taking on work where he could find it, all the while juggling school and the help expected of him in the fields. A week after turning sixteen, he'd bought himself a car—announced the purchase by dropping the keys in the middle of the supper table, told his father he'd made the down payment with his own money, that the monthly installments would come out of his earnings. He was used to things going his way. Now, for the first time, something had happened that couldn't be handled by facing it down, by squeezing in more hours for work, by a layout of hard-earned cash.

He'd been just thirteen when he had his first woman—a rancher's wife where he was helping with the cattle. She was pretty enough—looked to be thirty, thirty-five—invited him in one afternoon when the rancher had gone off somewhere and Jimmy Don was waiting for his father to pick him up. He'd been told he could pass for sixteen; he said seventeen when the rancher's wife asked. He learned a lot from her, learned the signs to look for in other women, kept his mouth shut about all of them, made up stories about made-up girls to cover with his friends.

And then Patsy.

AFTER the night she slapped him, he didn't see her for a week. She wouldn't come to the phone. After school one afternoon he tried the drugstore on Main Street, where she worked. Patsy disappeared into the back room and waited him out. By sunset on Friday, he was edgy with worry and anger. "Fuck it," he said and drove to her house. Her parents were nice people—and no match for Patsy, who would've made it clear he wasn't welcome. A minute of their muddle was all he could stand. "I'm sorry," he said. "I've got to see Patsy." He left them standing at the door and took the stairs up to her room. An old iron bedstead with a pink chenille spread. A dresser, the mirror edged with bric-a-brac. Patsy turned from the window. She would have seen him driving up, would have heard his voice downstairs.

In the week gone by, he hadn't thought once about what he might say. He'd only wanted to see Patsy. What he said, when the words came, was not pretty.

"I don't want this."

Patsy looked tired. She looked worried. Scared. But her words matched his for bluntness.

"You did your part to get it."

Jimmy Don's answer was what he willed to be true. "You can't have a baby in you."

"So I should get rid of it? Is that what you want?"

"I don't want this."

"*What,* then? Want to drive somewhere and have your way with me? Wouldn't have to use protection—that damage is done."

Outside, the tamped rumble of a car at the stop sign. A breath—and the engine revved, the driver taking on speed as laughter spilled into the dark. Patsy closed the window—a thump where frame met sill—and the voices were gone.

"I need some time," he said.

"What do you suppose that'll get you?"

Patsy drifted from the window to her dresser. She touched a dried corsage fading among the things on the mirror's frame. For a moment, Jimmy Don was certain he smelled carnations.

"If you do that," he said—a crazy hope, that she would get rid of it. "What you said—if you do that—what about after?"

By the look on her face, Patsy hadn't thought about after.

"What about us?" It was the wrong question. He knew that before it was out of his mouth.

"Us?" Patsy said, the word like an intake of breath, like a tonic she swallowed to strengthen the words that came next. "Go home, Jimmy Don. Find someone else to ruin."

ANOTHER week went by. He tried to reach Patsy at work. She hung up. Tried to reach her at home. She wouldn't come to the phone. Parked his car outside her house for hours on end. Nothing. At two on Saturday, her parents called, worried sick. Patsy had gone out the night before and hadn't come back. All morning they'd been calling her friends. They'd tried to reach Carter. No luck there. Jimmy Don was clearly a last resort; Patsy must've poisoned her folks against him.

He drove straight to the Geistweidts and questioned them for clues. They were no help at all, except to kindle the beginnings of dread. He drove to Carter's house. Neither of the cousins was there. Arlene was evasive, said she didn't know where her husband was or when he'd be back. She wasn't happy that Jimmy Don said he'd wait. When the phone rang, she jumped like a rabbit, closing the door on her way to answer it. He couldn't distinguish words, but Jimmy Don knew worry when he heard it. And he was persuasive. Within the hour, he had a street address in San Antonio, a room number.

A hundred miles later, he pulled up to a shabby motor court on the city's south side.

Carter answered his knock, a dim room behind him. A dresser top, its finish a pattern of pale circles where beer bottles and drink glasses had stood perspiring. A dingy window to the courtyard. A narrow bed, a rumpled, washed-out coverlet. Patsy's head on the pillow.

Jimmy Don crossed the room and went down on one knee at her side. She was so pale. He knew the answer to his question before he asked it.

"What have you done?"

Carter's voice behind him. "This was your call."

Jimmy Don crouched low at Patsy's side and waited for her to look at him. "Tell me you didn't," he said.

"You wanted it." Her voice was as weak as she looked, and there was a note in it he didn't want to hear. Loathing or its near kin.

Carter's voice behind him. "You aren't wanted here."

Jimmy Don turned, springing, and pinned Carter against the wall. Carter didn't try to get loose. He looked at Jimmy Don.

"We got rid of you," he said, and it was like when Patsy had slapped him—the stinging in his nose and eyes, the nearness of tears.

Jimmy Don let go. He turned to Patsy. "I'll stay," he said. "Carter can go."

"No," said Patsy.

He babbled a bit then, a series of promises delivered kneeling at her pillow. He'd be with her when she felt better. He'd make it up to her. They'd be together again.

To each one, Patsy mouthed a silent no.

"I love you," he said, nothing to lose now, knowing it was useless.

"Now you're gonna say it." Carter's voice again, sad now, no longer angry.

And Patsy. "It's too late for that."

"Go home," Carter said. "This is what you wanted."

III.

JIMMY DON SAT IN HIS car at the motor court until the neon arrow beside the highway started blinking. By the time he turned his key in the ignition, Robert and Dorene had stepped onto the floor at the Cotton Patch for their first dance in ages.

She was wearing the yellow dress, and whatever Robert might have felt three years ago, when Michael presented the fabric and pattern at the supper table, it looked forgotten now. In the car, as they pulled into the parking area, she'd adjusted the neckline so that it clung just off the shoulder.

"You're gonna raise some eyebrows," was all he said.

Inside, Michael trailed them to a table. "Save a number for me," he told her and drifted to the edges of the dance floor, hanging out there with others his age. Max was gone for the weekend, working cattle in place of Jimmy Don, who'd made the last minute arrangement and then gone running off God knows where. He'd been impossible lately.

Robert brought two beers from the concession stand, so cold, what with the ice they'd been plucked from, the first swallows almost hurt going down. They danced a waltz, afterwards dawdling as they made their way back, open-air voices from the tables and benches rising and falling and all jumbled together so that you couldn't hear any one person, all of them talking at the same time and nobody really listening to anybody else, just being part of something more than the words they tossed into the fray.

Several times Michael came and danced with Dorene. He'd inherited her love of dancing. He was smooth, effortless in his movements. At twelve, he was still short—a thin boy, light on his feet. He smiled and smiled dancing with her. She knew he gave himself credit for the dress, for the good times she would have wearing it.

The last dance of the evening was a waltz. Robert took her hand; he spun them in circles and circles as they rounded the floor. It might have been the beer—she'd had several—or the dizzying motions of the waltz. Or happiness—perhaps she'd forgotten how that felt. But circling, circling with Robert—*one* two three, *one* two three—Dorene felt as if she were dancing out of herself, and Robert with her, dancing out of whatever it was that had snared them, waltzing to the last song, no one wanting it to end, the band letting it play on and on. A blur of colors, faces, voices outside the circles they spun, her yellow dress swirling and swirling.

MIDNIGHT found Jimmy Don sitting in his car on a narrow rutted dirt lane that ran between fields to Agua Dulce Creek, a swath of curves, dry most of the year, that wound between his father's farm and Nopalito. In the months before, he had come here with Patsy. They'd spread an old blanket beneath the oaks along the watershed. After the drive from San Antonio, instead of going home, he'd driven county roads until he found his way here. The windows were down, the night air cool, the memory of being here with Patsy so strong he could put fingertips to his tongue and taste her there.

He arrived at the gate to the farm just as the lights in the house blinked out, his parents and Michael home from the dance and gone to bed. Not wanting to wake them or face his mother's worry, the questions she might ask, he switched off the headlights and pulled to the side of the lane just inside the gate. He leaned back in the seat. He wasn't surprised that he didn't doze.

THEIR dancing clothes discarded, their good nights said, his parents surrendered the house to a quiet so deep Michael knew they'd fallen asleep. He had the bedroom to himself—Jimmy Don gone from the bed they shared, Max's narrow single bed empty against the far windows. Michael lay wide awake atop the sheets. He felt that he was waiting—for what, he didn't know. While he lay there, he thought about the dance and his mother in the yellow dress. It was right there, he could see it through the open door to the bathroom where she'd made herself ready for bed. She'd put the dress on a hanger, left it hanging from a knob to the storage space above the bathroom closet. It was a pale shimmer in the moonlight spilling into the house.

They were asleep; the house was his. He tiptoed through the stillness to the dress. Even by the faint glow filtering into the dark, it was lovely, the fabric light as touch against the back of his hand as he lifted the skirt at the hem. Stretching up on tiptoe, he unhooked the hanger from its knob and held the dress against himself, feeling the weave against bare thighs, bare knees, bare shins.

He carried it into the bedroom, closing the door to the bathroom quietly behind, and stood before his grandmother's old dresser, the big mirror rising from it, his jockey shorts white against pale skin, the dress like amber in the mirror's muted light. Taking the dress from the hanger, he raised it over his head, slipped his wrists into the armholes, and let the cool cotton drop down over him. He straightened the skirt and tugged the neckline into place just off the shoulder. He was Michael and not Michael looking back at himself in the yellow dress. Reaching, he pulled the switch-chain on the lamp that sat on the dresser, yellow light spilling through the shade against yellow fabric, against rickrack blue and red and purple, against the pale, pale skin of Michael and not Michael.

Jimmy Don walked the lane beneath an almost full moon, the house quiet and dark before him. He was crossing the yard toward the back door, hackberry leaves shushing above him, when a light came on in the windows to his bedroom. He ducked behind the hackberry trunk and peered around.

Michael stood there looking in the mirror—steady, as if becalmed by what looked back—himself in the dress their mother had sewed for the dance tonight.

A day ago, seeing what he saw, Jimmy Don would have walked into the house and trounced his little brother. He didn't have it in him now. He whispered to himself, his brother's name, whispered, "Michael, Michael," not sure in the moment if he heard disapproval or wonder in his own voice.

He would have turned and walked back to his car, would have slept there. But a sound from elsewhere in the house drew his attention—a dark form at his parents' bedroom window, his mother pausing there and then fading toward her bedroom door, a habit she'd not put behind her, checking on her sleeping sons. More than once, coming in late, Jimmy Don had found her sitting bedside at his place, waiting, wanting to know that he was safely home. And now no way to warn Michael.

In the time it would have taken her to walk through the house, the door from the bathroom opened into the bedroom where Michael stood, their mother a dark shape where the door had been.

Michael turned and froze as surely as if some evil creature had cast a spell on him. Their mother stepped across the room and when she touched him, a calming hand—Jimmy Don knew this about her—when she touched Michael, he struck out at her, writhing, a brief silent struggle that stopped when Michael cried out, a short, sharp, wordless shout. For a moment, nothing. Then their father's voice calling from the dark of the bedroom their mother had left. She raised her head, like a deer testing the air. Then she turned and was gone. Moments later, her voice from the dark where their father had called, her tone reassuring. Finally, her shape at the window, and behind her, quiet.

Through the other window, in the light of the lamp on their grandmother's dresser, Michael tore at their mother's yellow dress, yanking it over his head and flinging the dress away from him. He crossed to the bathroom and closed the door there, walked back to the dresser and pulled the chain on the lamp. As dark flowed out and moonlight flowed in, Jimmy Don's eyes adjusted. Michael stood facing the mirror. He reached for the band of white that clothed him and, pushing down from the waist, stepped out of his jockey shorts and dropped them. He stood again facing the mirror, all of him pale, no patch of dark yet where his penis drooped.

The youngest son, the eldest, their mother—awake too late. Michael, fixed in place, as if he will not move, will not lie down to sleep. At the bedroom window opposite, Dorene, standing watch over the night. Beneath the hackberry tree, a witness, his face streaming tears. Behind him, from a tree out by the wash line, an owl calls. Michael turns toward the sound. Jimmy Don swivels behind the tree, his back to the trunk, his shadow absorbed by the dark there. He wonders when morning will come.

PETER LaBERGE

Harvest Elegy

We learn it starts in one line and continues
to the next. Father flips the seasons

in his electric skillet. Mother warms the rosary
beads in her palm. One morning, she learns

what her son does to the men
inside his adolescent head, how he makes them

stoop and fertilize until none of this pollen
that makes regret remains. Outside, this season

of crops has swelled, this desire devout and purple.
Father says we must sell it with the plums, but he cannot

pretend the world hasn't created this. Because
the men sing in the streets, because the notes slip,

shameless, into each other, I know I can
only jar this fruit, and never grow another.

In Defense of Driftwood

for Will Jardell

At midnight, I heard the bridge ask
to cross me, and I let it.

　　　　•

Driftwood fell in the river, then. *If nobody
catches it, do we call it fallen?*

No. We call it *born*. As in, *The boy
was born crooked.*

　　　　•

I cannot question this river
inside of me, so *yes, I wore the heels.*

I can only trawl to lift what I took
and weighed with stones.

　　　　•

I can't deepen the world without a second mouth.

Call to Worship

This winter I am breaking

                    every rule of winter. I wash
my body with scented soap. In my dreams

I dig to find the body

                    of a boy I kissed twice
behind the bales of my father's wheat.

Now that I have

                    I start to refill this plot
of ground, but no matter how much

I shovel, these moments buckle

                    the ground, knot the frost: *Once, I let
my face down into his river. Once, I filled his body with stones.*

KARINA BOROWICZ

In Its Body

The snow taps a pattern
on my skin. I always think of snow
as a living thing,

have always believed in its body,
that snow's silence is its own choosing.

The breath of snow.
Inaudible, but so is the breath of any wildness
to our ears.

This is the first day it has dared come so close
in a long time, and I'm not afraid.

Closer

When water
is the whole
body

like today

I tap my fingers
on yellow birch leaves
delicate petals
of corrosion
on the iron fence
stone wings
folded against stone
shoulders

Cold rain

good rain

drive me even closer

into the phosphorescence
of lichen

KEVIN PRUFER

Menhirs

I was lying on the couch
and outside rain kept falling
so I turned the page of my magazine
while Mary hummed in the bedroom,
changing the sheets.
On television, a man went on about
dead empires. What was he saying?
Piles of stones, long stone walls
winding through the green fields of,
I guessed England, then
several mysterious stone circles
in the center of which were—
I knew what they were called—
menhirs. The television was
muted and the man moved his lips
again, perfectly comfortable
among the stones and wind,
in his tweed jacket, his bright red tie.
Mary was still humming,
pushing the beds back into place.
Once again, the sheets were
clean and smelled of soap.
Outside, the rain came down
in vast populations and now
I was slipping into sleep,
raindrops exploding on the windows,
wind leaning into the walls. That week,
a young woman I knew slightly
had drowned. They'd towed her empty boat
through the storm. I must write her family,
I thought from far away. Then, a sense,
like a warm wind, settled against me:
we drift through time

the way trees drift through rain.
We hold none of it. We hold
none of it. I felt terrified
in the bright room. On TV,
the man was still talking.
Mary pointed the remote control at him
as if to change the channel.
For a moment longer
the menhirs glowed in the sunset.

Love Poem: Just Then

Just as the young man pulled the Glock from his jacket
and aimed it at the cashier's head,

at the very moment he balanced the gun just so,
but before he could say a word,

while outside the sun slipped from a cloud
and brightened the parking lot's windshields,

just as the old man at the register realized
exactly what was going to happen next,

to him, to his head, the way it would feel,
concussive, just then, far away,

you lay in bed that Sunday morning,
having just made love, the sound of him

washing himself in the bathroom, his gentle cough,
just as you contemplated opening the blinds

to let a little sun in, just then, the sun
holding its breath, stillness, stillness, the cool

noise of water, just then I was writing
about how I missed you and wanted you back,

how could I not have you back?
how could I not take you back?

just then, that man opened the door
and walked right into my sunlit poem

and drew his gun on the old clerk
who held up his hands, said, *Stop,*

I'll give you whatever you want. I'll give you
everything you want—

and even the bullet, snug in its chamber,
couldn't believe what would happen next,

what it would become: a sunburst, an idea,
a sort of pathway.

JONATHAN WEINERT

Tilted City

The things we passed by every day
outlasted us: comb-teeth scattered
in the gravel, bits of plastic from a laptop.

When our walls came down our shadows
vanished: centuries of slow corrosion,
not the action of our hit-to-kill

materiel. Before our windows all went black
we grew so tired; we wanted clouds for beds
and hills for pillows, valleys

where the very wolves would warm us
and adore us.

•

We walked our sons to parks down quiet lanes
and held them when their fear and shame
seemed everything.

We watched their unoffending legs
go flashing down the playgrounds
—boys: those keepers of the cold

white flowers, deep rememberers,
who stepped on grass and laughed,
their girl-limbs bright and pliable

as they climbed the blood-red rungs
and shuddered at the heights.

•

We wanted beauty in ourselves,
and sleep. Some wanted blood.
We wanted beauty in ourselves

and others' blood. We wanted rest,
and others' grief. We wanted terror
elsewhere, peace at home, the ceaseless

hiss of rain on leaves. The sky kept
going overhead, a lesson in exchange
we never learned. The roadbeds trembled

on the earth's hot core, our shadows
lay down in the streets and slept.

•

We sent our circuitry over all the earth.
We sent our weapons, our machines.
Inside, we still were wet and animal;

inside, our boys were wet and animal,
and they climbed on metal bars
and shouted at the darkness. Every face

a cold white flower, hands electric
with the fervor of their play,
great creators of the moment,

establishers of paradise, fallers-down-on-grass,
fierce criers, pedallers, untried cadets.

•

We sent our certainty over all the earth.
We sent our idols, our latrines.
Inside, we still were dark and liminal;

inside, our boys were dark and liminal,
and they dreamed on blocks of foam
of seas they'd never seen,

of beaked and big-eyed swimmers,
and they'd wake up finned and razor-toothed,
they worshipped at the Church of Red

Imaginary Creatures, stingray boys in PJs
biding time until the sirens called their names.

•

Now the sifters' nervous fingers find our stuff:
ballpoint pen caps, cellphone chipsets,
diapers, filings, clickers, toilet seats,

the petrified remains of hot-drink cups
and plastic bags, palimpsests of ads
and patents, hood medallions, dipsticks,

gaskets, nylons, Scrabble pieces, septic tanks,
Kindle cases, keypads, mounded bones of dogs
and cats, cables, jackets, piping, Tyvek,

copper flashing, slabs with writings on them,
diamonds, poisons, gold from domes . . .

•

We slept while fifteen hundred years
passed over us. No one living
knows our names, or what we saw,

or how it was with us. The sifters,
bending to their cuts and fills,
expose and comb and analyze,

but cannot speak to us.
So much obliterated love,
the scraped uncertain contexts,

the cold white flowers of our ankle bones
shining from the dirt.

JOHN POCH

Negatives

You don't really know a person
till you've seen a dead one.

The shadow of the earth
on its atmosphere is called the terminator,

and sometimes the night comes on
like a crow eating crow unaware.

There's no kind of sad
like dead kid sad, we all agreed.

The maggot is no worse than the fly,
we disagreed.

The photograph is an image
of God creating man in his image,

and this is why it haunts:
it gives life and takes it

away. The negative of a negative
is all there is to look at.

Bios

PAIGE ACKERSON-KIELY's most recent collection of poetry is *My Love Is a Dead Arctic Explorer* (Ahsahta, 2012). She lives in rural Vermont and works at a homeless shelter.

ROBERT ARCHAMBEAU's books include *The Poet Resigns: Poetry in a Difficult Word* (U of Akron Press, 2013), *Laureates and Heretics: Six Careers in American Poetry* (U of Notre Dame Press, 2010), and *The Kafka Sutra* (MadHat Press, 2015; forthcoming). He teaches at Lake Forest College.

BRUCE BOND is the author of fourteen books, including five forthcoming: *Immanent Distance: Poetry and the Metaphysics of the Near at Hand* (U of Michigan Press); *For the Lost Cathedral* (LSU Press); *Black Anthem* (U of Tampa Press), which won the Tampa Review Prize; *Sacrum* (Four Way Books); and *The Other Sky* (Etruscan Press). He is Regents Professor at the University of North Texas.

KARINA BOROWICZ is the author of two poetry collections: *Proof* (Codhill Press, 2014) and *The Bees Are Waiting* (Marick Press, 2012), which won the Eric Hoffer Award for Poetry and was named a Mist-Read by the Massachusetts Center for the Book. Recent work has been featured in *Green Mountains Review, Pleiades,* and NPR's *Writer's Almanac.* Visit her website at karinaborowicz.com.

LAURA CESARCO EGLIN has published three poetry collections in Uruguay. For more information, see page 125.

MARTHA COLLINS' eighth book of poems, *Admit One: An American Scrapbook,* will be published by the University of Pittsburgh Press in early 2016. Collins is also the author of seven earlier books of poetry, most recently *Day Unto Day* (Milkweed, 2014), *White Papers* (U of Pittsburgh Press, 2012), and *Blue Front* (Graywolf Press, 2006), and co-translator of four collections of Vietnamese poetry. She is editor-at-large for *FIELD* magazine and an editor for the Oberlin College Press.

LINDSEY DRAGER has published prose in *Black Warrior Review, Gulf Coast, Kenyon Review Online, Quarterly West,* and elsewhere. An editor for Starcherone Books and the *Denver Quarterly,* she has received residencies from the Kimmel Harding Nelson Center for the Arts and the Vermont Studio Center. Her novel, *The Sorrow Proper* is forthcoming from Dzanc Books in 2015.

JEHANNE DUBROW is the author of four poetry collections, including *Red Army Red* and *Stateside* (Northwestern UP, 2012 and 2010). In 2015, University of New Mexico Press will publish her fifth book, *The Arranged Marriage*. Her work has recently appeared in *The New England Review*, *Prairie Schooner*, and *The Southern Review*. She directs the Rose O'Neill Literary House and teaches at Washington College.

BRANDEL FRANCE de BRAVO's essays have appeared or are forthcoming in the *Bellingham Review*, *Better*, *Fourth Genre*, *Seneca Review* and elsewhere. She is the author of two books of poetry—*Mother, Loose* (Accents Publishing, 2014) and *Provenance* (Washington Writers, 2008)—the editor of *Mexican Poetry Today: 20/20 Voices* (Shearsman Books, 2010), and co-author of a parenting book. She works for a consumer health organization in Washington, D.C.

ROGER GREENWALD grew up in New York and lives in Toronto. He has won two Canadian Broadcasting Corporation Literary Awards (for poetry and travel literature) and many translation awards for his numerous translations from Danish and Norwegian. He has published two books of poems, most recently *Slow Mountain Train* (Tiger Bark Press, 2015).

MARK HALLIDAY teaches at Ohio University. His sixth book of poems, *Thresherphobe*, was published in 2013 by the U of Chicago Press.

DAVID HERNANDEZ's most recent collection of poems is *Hoodwinked* (Sarabande Books, 2011). His awards include a Pushcart Prize, an NEA Literature Fellowship in Poetry, and the Kathryn A. Morton Prize. His poems have appeared in *Ploughshares*, *The Missouri Review*, *Field*, *The Southern Review*, and *The Best American Poetry 2013*. Visit his website at www.davidahernandez.com.

CHRISTINA HESSELHOLDT is the author of eleven books in Danish. For more information about her work, see page 105.

TONY HOAGLAND is the author of five poetry collections, most recently *Application for Release from the Dream: Poems* (Graywolf Press, 2015). Finalist for the National Book Critics Circle Award and winner of the James Laughlin Award, he teaches at the University of Houston.

JESSE LEE KERCHEVAL is the author of fifteen books of poetry, fiction, and nonfiction—most recently the novel *My Life as a Silent Movie* (Indiana UP, 2013), the novella *Brazil* (Cleveland State UP, 2010), and the poetry collection *Cinema Muto* (Southern Illinois UP, 2009). She is currently editing *América Invertida: A Bilingual Anthology of Younger Uruguayan Poets* (U of New Mexico Press, forthcoming).

JILL KHOURY's poems have appeared or are forthcoming in numerous journals, including *Arsenic Lobster*, *Inter|rupture*, *RHINO*, and *Stone Highway Review*. Her chapbook *Borrowed Bodies* was released by Pudding House Press in 2009. You can find her at jillkhoury.com.

LISA KO's fiction has appeared in *Narrative*, *Apogee Journal*, *Brooklyn Review*, *The Asian Pacific American Journal*, and elsewhere. She has been awarded fellowships from the New York Foundation for the Arts, the MacDowell Colony, and Hawthornden Castle. "Pat + Sam" is part of a collection of linked short stories. She is also working on a novel.

The recipient of the Kingsley-Tufts Award, **JOHN KOETHE** has published numerous poetry collections, most recently *Ninety-Fifth Street* (Harper Perennial, 2009), *ROTC Kills* (2012), and the forthcoming *The Swimmer* (2016). He is Emeritus Professor of Philosophy at the University of Wisconsin Milwaukee.

MARY KURYLA's stories have received The Pushcart Prize and have appeared or are forthcoming in *Alaska Quarterly Review*, *Epoch*, *Greensboro Review*, and *Witness*. Kuryla is the author, with Eugene Yelchin, of several children's books, including *Ghost Files: The Haunting Truth* (2008) from HarperCollins.

PETER LaBERGE is the author of the chapbook *Hook* (Sibling Rivalry Press, 2015). His poetry appears in *Beloit Poetry Journal*, *Redivider*, *Best New Poets 2014*, *DIAGRAM*, and *Indiana Review*, among others. He recently co-edited *Poets on Growth* (Math Paper Press, 2015) and serves as the founder & editor-in-chief of *The Adroit Journal*. He lives in Philadelphia, where he is an undergraduate student at the University of Pennsylvania.

KEITH LEONARD's first poetry collection, *Ramshackle Ode*, is forthcoming from Houghton Mifflin Harcourt in 2016. The recipient of fellowships from the Bread Loaf and Sewanee Writers' Conferences, he teaches at Indiana University.

Prominent Uruguayan writer **CIRCE MAIA** is the author of nine books of poetry and a novel. For more information, see page 125.

DAVID MEISCHEN has short stories in *The Gettysburg Review*, *Bellingham Review*, *The Evansville Review*, *Valparaiso Fiction Review*, and elsewhere. His poetry has appeared in *The Southern Review* and *Southern Poetry Review*, among others. Co-editor of *Wingbeats* and *Wingbeats II*, poetry-writing exercises from Dos Gatos Press, he won the Writers' League of Texas Manuscript Contest in Mainstream Fiction, 2011, and the Talking Writing Fiction Contest, 2012.

TYLER MILLS is the author of the poetry collection *Tongue Lyre* (Southern Illinois UP, 2013), and her poems have appeared in *The New Yorker*, *Poetry*, *Boston Review*, *Georgia Review*, and elsewhere. She is editor-in-chief of *The Account* and teaches at new Mexico Highlands University.

JEFFREY MORGAN is the author of the poetry collection *Crying Shame* (BlazeVOX Books, 2011), and his poems have appeared in *Bat City Review*, *Pleiades*, *Third Coast*, *West Branch*, and elsewhere.

KATHRYN NUERNBERGER's poetry collections are *Rag & Bone* (Elixir Press, 2011) and *The End of Pink* (BOA Editions, 2016; forthcoming). She teaches at the University of Central Missouri and edits Pleiades Press.

Work by MARC PALTRINERI has appeared in such journals as *The Laurel Review*, *PANK*, *Washington Square*, *The Green Mountains Review*, among others. A graduate of the MFA program at the University of New Hampshire, he lives near Iowa City.

JOHN POCH's most recent book, *Fix Quiet* (St. Augustine's Press, 2015), won the 2014 New Criterion Poetry Prize. His work has appeared in many journals, including *Yale Review*, *Poetry*, *Paris Review*, and *Agni*. He teaches in the creative writing program at Texas Tech University.

KEVIN PRUFER's sixth poetry collection is *How He Loved Them* (Four Way Books, forthcoming). He has coedited multiple volumes, including, most recently, the forthcoming *Into English: An Anthology of Multiple Tranlsations* (Graywolf, 2016) and *Literary Publishing in the 21ˢᵗ Century* (Milkweed, 2016). The recipient of four Pushcart Prizes and multiple *Best American Poetry* selections, Prufer teaches at the University of Houston.

JAMES RICHARDSON's most recent collection is *During* (Copper Canyon, 2015). The recipient of the 2011 Jackson Prize for Poetry, Richardson's previous books include *By the Numbers* (2010), a finalist for the National Book Award, and *Interglacial* (Ausable, 2004), a finalist for the National Book Critics Circle Award.

POLLY ROSENWAIKE's fiction has been published in *Prairie Schooner*, *Indiana Review*, *New Delta Review*, *New England Review*, *The O. Henry Prize Stories 2013*, and elsewhere. Her book reviews and essays have appeared in *The New York Times Book Review*, *The San Francisco Chronicle*, and *The Millions*. She teaches creative writing at Eastern Michigan University.

RON PAUL SALUTSKY is the author of the poetry collection *Romeo Bones* (Steel Toe Books, 2013). His translation of Karen Wild's *Anti-Ferule* is forthcoming from Toad Press.

LAUREN SHAPIRO is the author of the poetry collection *Easy Math* (Sarabande Books, 2013) and co-editor of *The New Census: An Anthology of Contemporary American Poetry* (Rescue Press, 2013). She teaches at Carnegie Mellon University.

ED SKOOG is the author of two books of poems, *Mister Skylight* (2009) and *Rough Day* (2013), both published by Copper Canyon Press. *Rough Day* won the 2014 Washington State Book Award. He lives in Seattle.

LAURA STOTT is the author of the book of poems, *In the Museum of Coming and Going* (New Issues Poetry & Prose, 2014). She received her MFA from Eastern Washington University and her poems have appeared in various journals, including *Bellingham Review*, *Hayden's Ferry Review*, *Cutbank*, *Quarterly West*, and elsewhere. She teaches at Weber State University in Utah.

From Nashville, **ANNA B. SUTTON** received her MFA from UNC Wilmington and a James Merrill fellowship from the Vermont Studio Center. Her work has appeared or is forthcoming in *Third Coast*, *Quarterly West*, *DIAGRAM*, and other journals. She is co-founder of The Porch Writers' Collective, web editor at One Pause Poetry, poetry editor at *Dialogist*, and a reader at *Gigantic Sequins*.

FIONA SZE-LORRAIN, a *zheng* harpist living in Paris, is the author of three poetry collections—most recently *The Ruined Elegance* (Princeton UP, 2015)—and the translator of collections by Bai Hua, Yu Xiang, Lan Lan, and Zhang Zao, all published by Zephyr Press. Her translation of Yi Lu's *Sea Summit* is forthcoming from Milkweed in 2016.

JULIE MARIE WADE is the author of eight books of poetry and nonfiction, including two forthcoming poetry collections: *SIX* (Red Hen Press, 2015) and *Catechism: A Love Story* (Noctuary Press, 2016). She teaches at Florida International University.

JONATHAN WEINERT is the author of the chapbook *Thirteen Small Apostrophes* (Back Pages Publishers, 2013) and Nightboat Poetry Prize winner *In the Mode of Disappearance* (Nightboat Books, 2008). He is coeditor of *Until Everything Is Continuous Again: American Poets on the Recent Work of W.S. Merwin* (WordFarm, 2012).

KAREN WILD is the author of a poetry collection, *Anti-Férula*, in Uruguay, which is forthcoming in English translation from Toad Hollow Press. For more information, see page 125.

STEFANIE WORTMAN's first book of poems, *In the Permanent Collection*, was selected for the Vassar Miller Prize and published by the University of North Texas Press in 2014. Her poems and essays have appeared in *Yale Review*, *Michigan Quarterly Review*, *Boston Review*, and other publications. She lives in Rhode Island.

The author of five poetry collections, **YI LU** is a leading contemporary Chinese poet. For more information, see page 15.

Required Reading

(Issue 21)

(Each issue we ask that our contributors recommend up to three recent titles.
What follows is the list generated by this issue's contributors.)

Elisa Albert, *After Birth* (Stefanie Wortman)

David Baker, *Scavenger Loop* (Tyler Mills)

Ellen Bass, *Like a Beggar* (Laura Stott)

Sandra Beasley, *Count the Waves* (David Hernandez)

Aaron Belz, *Glitter Bomb* (Robert Archambeau)

Oliver Bendorf, *The Spectral Wilderness* (Keith Leonard)

Malachi Black, *Storm Toward Morning* (John Poch)

Craig Blais, *About Crows* (Ron Paul Salutsky)

Marianne Boruch, *Cadaver, Speak* (David Hernandez)

Kimberly Burwick, *Goodnight Brother* (Julie Marie Wade)

Rocío Cerón, *Diorama*, trans. Anna Rosenwong (Jesse Lee Kercheval)

Victoria Chang, *The Boss* (Jeffrey Morgan)

Cathy Linh Che, *Split* (Jehanne Dubrow)

George David Clark, *Reveille* (John Poch)

Killarney Clary, *Shadow of a Cloud but No Cloud* (Ed Skoog)

Jennifer Clement, *Prayers for the Stolen* (Brandel France de Bravo)

Cecelia Corrigan, *Titanic* (Robert Archambeau)

Robert Crawford, *Young Eliot: From St. Louis to The Waste Land* (John Koethe)

Charles D'Ambrosio, *Loitering: New and Collected Stories* (Mary Kuryla)

John Darnielle, *Wolf in White Van* (Jill Khoury)

Lydia Davis, *Can't and Won't: Stories* (John Poch)

Olena Kalytiak Davis, *Poem She Didn't Write and Other Poems* (Ed Skoog)

Kendra DeColo, *Thieves in the Afterlife* (Keith Leonard, Tyler Mills)

Jill Alexander Essbaum, *Haufrau: A Novel* (David Meischen)

Angie Estes, *Enchantée* (Bruce Bond)

Tarfia Faizullah, *Seam* (Peter LaBerge)

Katie Ford, *Blood Lyrics* (Bruce Bond, David Hernandez)

John Gallaher, *In a Landscape* (Marc Paltrineri)

Sarah Galvin, *The Three Einsteins* (Ed Skoog)

Ross Gay, *Catalog of Unabashed Gratitude* (Keith Leonard)

Martin Gayford, *A Bigger Message: Conversations with David Hockney* (Jonathan Weinert)

Douglas Goetsch, *Nameless Boy* (Mark Halliday)

Ray Gonzalez, *Soul Over Lightning* (Kathryn Nuernberger)

Jorie Graham, *From the New World: Poems 1976-2014* (Martha Collins)

Alfred Starr Hamilton, *A Dark Dreambox of Another Kind* (Marc Paltrineri)

Langdon Hammer, *James Merrill: Life and Art* (John Koethe)

Daisy Hernandez, *A Cup of Water under My Bed* (Julie Marie Wade)

H. L. Hix, *As Much As, If Not More Than* (Jonathan Weinert)

Tony Hoagland, *Application for Release from the Dream* (Kevin Prufer)

George Hodgman, *Bettyville: A Memoir* (David Meischen)

Tom Holmes, *The Cave* (Laura Stott)

Nick Hornby, *Ten Years in the Tub* (Polly Rosenwaike)

Bethany Schultz Hurst, *Miss Lost Nation* (Laura Stott)

Alta Ifland, *Elegy for a Fabulous World* (Roger Greenwald)

Leslie Jamison, *The Empathy Exams* (Brandel France de Bravo)

TJ Jarrett, *Zion* (Anna B. Sutton)

Sarah Eliza Johnson, *Bone Map* (Kathryn Nuernberger)

Anna Journey, *Vulgar Remedies* (Peter LaBerge)

Laura Kasischke, *The Infinitesimals* (Polly Rosenwaike)

Nick Lantz, *How to Dance as the Roof Caves In* (Jesse Lee Kercheval)

Dorothea Lasky, *Rome* (Lauren Shapiro)

Claude Lecouteux, *The Tradition of Household Spirits: Ancestral Lore and Practices* (Mary Kuryla)

Yiyun Li, *Kinder Than Solitude* (Lisa Ko)

Frannie Lindsay, *Our Vanishing* (Karina Borowicz)

Sarah Lindsay, *Debt to the Bone-Eating Snotflower* (Mark Halliday)

Teddy Macker, *This World* (Karina Borowicz)

Circe Maia, *Invisible Bridge/El puente invisible: Selected Poems*, trans. Jesse Lee Kercheval (Ron Paul Salutsky)

Sally Wen Mao, *Mad Honey Symposium* (Jill Khoury)

Adrian Matejka, *The Big Smoke* (Jeffrey Morgan)

Shane McCrae, *Forgiveness Forgiveness* (Lauren Shapiro)

Philip Metres, *Sand Opera* (Jehanne Dubrow)

Erika Meitner, *Copia* (Jehanne Dubrow)

Stephen S. Mills, *A History of the Unmarried* (Julie Marie Wade)

Ander Monson, *Letter to a Future Lover: Marginalia, Errata, Secrets, Inscriptions, and Other Ephemera Found in Libraries* (Lindsey Drager)

john mortara, *some planet* (Anna B. Sutton)

Simone Muench, *Wolf Centos* (Jill Khoury)

Maggie Nelson, *The Argonauts* (Brandel France de Bravo)

January Gill O'Neill, *Misery Islands* (Martha Collins)

Caryl Pagel, *Twice Told* (Kevin Prufer)

Gregory Pardlo, *Digest* (Kevin Prufer)

V. Penelope Pelizzon, *Whose Flesh Is Flame, Whose Bone Is Time* (Martha Collins)

Angela Pelster, *Limber* (Marc Paltrineri)

Alejandra Pizarnik, *Extracting the Stone of Madness: Poems 1962-1972*, trans. Yvette Siegert (Jesse Lee Kercheval)

Stanley Plumly, *The Immortal Evening: A Legendary Dinner with Keats, Wordsworth, and Lamb* (Tyler Mills)

Kevin Prufer, *Churches* (Mark Halliday)

Claudia Rankine, *Citizen: An American Lyric* (Martha Collins)

Matt Rasmussen, *Black Aperture: Poems* (Jeffrey Morgan)

Bushra Rehman, *Corona* (Lisa Ko)

Michael Robbins, *The Second Sex* (Robert Archambeau)

Gabriel Roth, *The Unknowns: A Novel* (Polly Rosenwaike)

Tomasz Różycki, *Colonies*, trans. Mira Rosenthal (Roger Greenwald)

Mary Ruefle, *Trances of the Blast* (Jonathan Weinert)

Joanna Ruocco, *Dan* (Lindsey Drager)

Chika Sagawa, *The Collected Poems of Chika Sagawa*, trans. Sawako Nakayasu (Lauren Shapiro)

Judith Schalansky, *Pocket Atlas of Remote Islands: Fifty Islands I Have Not Visited and Never Will* (Paige Ackerson-Kiely)

Gjertrud Schnackenberg, *Heavenly Questions* (Roger Greenwald)

Richard Siken, *War of the Foxes* (Kathryn Nuernberger)

Danez Smith, *[insert] boy* (Peter LaBerge)

Susan Steinberg, *Spectacle* (Mary Kuryla)

Christina Stoddard, *Hive* (Anna B. Sutton)

Mark Strand, *Collected Poems* (Fiona Sze-Lorrain)

A. K. Summers, *Pregnant Butch: Nine Long Months Spent in Drag* (Stefanie Wortman)

Allison Titus, *The Arsonist's Song Has Nothing to Do with Fire* (Paige Ackerson-Kiely)

Justin Torres, *We the Animals* (Lisa Ko)

Barbara Ungar, *Immortal Medusa* (Karina Borowicz)

Jane Unrue, *Love Hotel* (Lindsey Drager)

Lee Upton, *Bottle the Bottles the Bottles the Bottles* (Stefanie Wortman)

Mark Wunderlich, *The Earth Avails* (Bruce Bond)

The Copper Nickel Editors' Prizes
(est. 2015)

Past Winners

spring 2015

Michelle Oakes, poetry
Donovan Ortega, prose

In celebration of 30 years of publication, we are pleased to announce a special e-book anthology comprising 12 of our favorite stories, together for the first time.

The Best Stories from

BOULEVARD

1985-2015 • Volume 1

Edited by Richard Burgin
with Jessica Rogen

Steve **Barthelme**

Jonathan **Baumbach**

Chris **Cefalu**

Stephen **Dixon**

Robert **Dow**

Giles **Harvey**

Alice **Mattison**

Joyce Carol **Oates**

Elizabeth **Orsndorff**

Melanie **Sumner**

Anthony **Varallo**

Marc **Watkins**

Anthology $10 • Anthology + Print Subscription $20
Anthology + Digital Subscription $17

For more information and to order go to
www.boulevardmagazine.org/anthology.html

Boulevard has been called "one of the half-dozen best literary journals"
by Poet Laureate Daniel Hoffman in *The Philadelphia Inquirer*

FORTHCOMING AUTUMN 2015

the Southern Review

POETRY

Aliki Barnstone, Fleda Brown, Anders Carlson-Wee, Brittany Cavallaro,
Jona Colson, Dan Encarnacion, Alan Feldman, Gary Gildner, Alen Hamza,
Jeffrey Harrison, Jenneva Kayser, David Kirby, Jacqueline Kolosov,
Sydney Lea, Katherine Mitchell, Alison Pelegrin, Charlotte Pence,
David Petruzelli, Anna Lena Phillips, Charles Rafferty, Philip Schultz,
Floyd Skloot, Jane Springer, David St. John, Ryan Teitman,
Anne Pierson Wiese, David Wojahn, Katie Bowler Young

FICTION

Steve Amick, Matthew Baker, Erin Flanagan, Nick Holdstock,
Cyrstal Kim, Ted Wheeler

NONFICTION

Bonnie Costello, Lance Larsen, Jacqueline Lyons

VISUAL ART

artworks by Alison Elizabeth Taylor

FALL 2015 POETRY

from

milkweed
editions

ADA LIMÓN
Bright Dead Things

———

YI LU
Sea Summit
Translated from the Chinese by Fiona Sze-Lorrain

———

NANCY REDDY
Double Jinx
2014 National Poetry Series Selection

———

JENNIFER WILLOUGHBY
Beautiful Zero
2015 Lindquist & Vennum Prize for Poetry Winner

COPPERNICKEL

subscription rates

For regular folks:

one year (two issues)—$20
two years (four issues)—$35
three years (six issues)—$45
five years (ten issues)—$60

For student folks:

one year (two issues)—$15
two years (four issues)—$23
three years (six issues)—$32
five years (ten issues)—$50

For more information, visit: www.copper-nickel.org.

To go directly to subscriptions
visit: www.regonline.com/coppernickelsubscriptions.

To order back issues, call 303-556-4026
or email wayne.miller@ucdenver.edu.